Redhill Rococo

REDHILL ROCOCO

Shena Mackay

HEINEMANN · LONDON

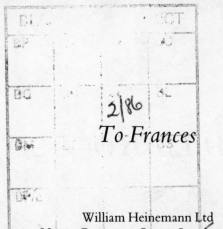

To·Frances

William Heinemann Ltd
10 Upper Grosvenor Street, London W1X 9PA
LONDON   MELBOURNE   TORONTO
JOHANNESBURG   AUCKLAND

First published 1986
Copyright © Shena Mackay 1986
SBN 434 44046 9

01170276

The author wishes to acknowledge
the assistance of the Arts Council of
Great Britain.

Photoset by Rowland Phototypesetting Ltd
Bury St Edmunds, Suffolk
Printed and bound in Great Britain by
Billings Ltd, Worcester

ONE

'REDHILL. This is Redhill. The train now at platform three is for . . .'

A boy stepped down from the train and stood on the platform, dazzled by the shimmering car park, the gilded hands of the dead asylum clock, the *Surrey Mirror* building, a glittering cube of golden glass in the early morning sun that illumined the town below him, made a halo of his hair and pearlised the prison pallor of his face. He noted a sign that warned 'REDHILL EXHAUSTS AND TYRES' as he made his way to the station forecourt where a semi-circle of mini-cabs dozed like basking sharks.

Not far away, Pearl Slattery wound a last violet skein of icing sugar. The air was drenched with roses and vanilla; her night's work was done; the day shift was clattering into the sweet factory. Pearl hung up her white coat and cap. *Aves atque vales* flew about like parakeets as she hurried into the street with her heavy handbag. A few coloured nonpareils spangled her hair. She arrived at her broken gate as a car pulled away leaving a pale youth on the pavement. She thought that the driver blew him a kiss, but of course this could not have been.

'Mrs Slattery?'

'Yes.'

'My name's Luke Ribbons. I believe your husband wrote to you about me . . .'

'Oh yes. You'd better come in.'

He followed her into the front garden. Big indiscreet roses flung themselves after them and fell back in an expense of petals and dew. They passed between two stone pineapples, climbed three shallow mossy steps and entered a dim hall. Mrs Slattery was speaking to him but her words were sucked into the buzz of a hoover elsewhere in the house. Luke's head struck a plastic chandelier, throwing a necklace of cheap rainbows over the ceiling. The hoover was drowned by music from a radio as they came into the kitchen.

As Luke lounged awkwardly against the wall he saw a little girl, in T-shirt and pants, half sitting, half kneeling on a stool at the table, reading; a spoon loaded with Rice Krispies poised in the air, dripping a stream of sugary milk on to her comic. Mrs Slattery upturned her handbag and a heap of sweets and chocolates, pink and green and silver, violets and roses, golden hearts and bloomy squares of Turkish delight poured on to the table.

'Oh, hello Mum, are you home?'

The child dropped her spoon with a soggy splash into the bowl and resumed reading, while her fingers, like a skilful crab searching among pebbles, clawed around for a choice chocolate.

'This is my youngest, Tiffany.' She kissed the top of the child's spiky head.

'Tiffany, say hello to Mr Ribbons. He's a friend of your father's.'

'Ribbons!' Tiffany choked and giggled, displaying chocolate teeth which her mouth had not yet grown to fit. 'Ribbons!' She sprayed milk over the table.

Luke was thinking that her name was much sillier than his; a silly taffeta or reproduction lampshade of a name.

'Don't be so rude, Tiffany. People can't help their names. I almost said "your late father" then, funny isn't it?' Mrs

2

Slattery added in an aside to Luke. She pulled back a chair and slumped into it. Her legs were bare; she eased off the heel of one shoe with the toe of the other; they were of emerald satin with square diamanté buckles clinging riskily to loose black stitches. She wriggled her toes.

'How is the old buzzard, then? Jack, I mean.'

She pulled a wine bottle from the cluttered table and put it to her mouth.

'Yuk.' She wiped away a bitter dreg.

'He's . . .'

'Fancy some breakfast? A bit of fried bread?'

Upstairs, Cherry Slattery was preparing a room for the new lodger. She bashed the vacuum cleaner under the bed, hitting a pile of old shoes. If she was a cherry, it was the Napoleon variety; under her tousled yellow curls a flush mantled her fair skin and a curse flew from her red lips as the hoover, from humour or spite, seized her exiguous nightdress in its plastic trunk and twisted it into a tight knot. She wrenched free, kicked off the switch and yanked out the plug.

She burst into the kitchen.

'I don't see why it always has to be me that – oh!'

She stood panting in her short nightdress, grey cotton sprinkled with greyer flowers, glaring at Luke Ribbons eating fried bread. He stood up greasily.

'Well, I hope you find your room to your satisfaction!'

'I hope I haven't put you to any inconvenience . . .'

'Oh, no, I just love – And those are my knickers! Get them off!'

She lunged at her sister, who fled, to the sound of screams off-stage.

Luke sat down again. He looked inquiringly at Mrs Slattery.

'My other daughter, Cherry.'

Her fried breakfast had sent her into a torpor. She wondered if her arm looked older than it had yesterday, and dismissed it as a trick of the light. She took a small round mirror from her bag and sighed.

'I don't really look like this,' she explained, 'I'm much

thinner, really. Trouble is, I've put on a bit of weight so it makes me look fatter than I am.'

'I see.'

'You look as if you could do with a bit of fattening up,' she added, a touch jealously. 'Didn't they feed you in that place?'

'Oh yes. It was mostly stodge though. You should see old Jack . . .'

He stopped, embarrassed that his words might be taken as an accusation. She had not been to visit her husband at all during his latest sentence for petty crime. Cherry re-entered, trim as a geometry set in her navy blue school uniform, followed by Tiffany in a cobbled mini-skirt.

'Is Sean up yet?' asked their mother.

'He went out early.'

'That's not like him. Tiffany, take your jacket, it's going to rain later.'

'No it isn't.'

'He had to go and see about that YTS scheme.'

'Don't argue. Take your jacket.'

'I can't.'

'Of course you can. Don't be so stupid.'

'Oh, come on, Tiffany. We'll be late!'

Cherry dragged a jacket from a heap of clothes and flung it at her sister. It fell to the floor.

'I can't wear a skin'ead jacket with a post-punk skirt, can I?' shouted Tiffany as she ran from the room. Their mother lifted a hand in a dispirited wave as they passed the window. The faded head of a dried flower fell from a vase on the mantelpiece; an immortelle belied its name.

'Well, I suppose I'd better get this place cleared up . . .'

She built a higgledy-piggledy pile of plates and knives and forks and dumped it in the sink and, satisfied, or defeated, sat down and lit a cigarette.

'Want one?'

She threw the pack at him, and a slick lighter like a lipstick.

'Mrs Slattery . . .'

'You may as well call me Pearl.'

4

'Thank you. Are you sure it's all right, you putting me up, I mean. It's very kind of you . . . I'll start looking for a job right away. I can't . . .'

He broke off as a youth of about his own age was supported in by two others.

'Sean!'

'He collapsed outside the Job Centre again.'

Dismissed by a glare, the bearers melted away.

Sean sank on to a stool. His fair hair was tinged with pink, so that his head, bowed between his hands, was a daisy with pink-tipped petals.

'Mum,' he croaked, 'do us a bit of fried bread.'

A huge yawn swelled Luke's face; he could not hide it.

'Shall I show you your room? You could rest up for a bit.'

He nodded.

As they went out Sean looked at him. Luke saw the question he had dreaded issuing from his mouth.

'What was you done for?'

'Sub-post office,' he muttered, manufacturing another yawn and exiting under its impetus.

When Pearl left him he lay down on the bed in a heavy scent pouring through the open window and a few moments later music from Sean's stereo pounded him to sleep.

The gun was small, the ammunition damp, and yet . . .

It was hardly the crime of the century, nor yet the crime of the week, even in the suburban sub-zero street where the tiny sub-post office in which it was perpetrated was sited. It had been knocked off the front page of the local paper by an accident involving three coach loads of pensioners on their way to a matinée of *Puss in Boots* at the Ashcroft Theatre. The coincidence of this disaster and the fact that his victims were also in the twilight of their lives went hard with Luke.

If his father had not sent him to buy stamps that day, if he had instead roused himself from the fug of his study where he sat like a frazzled marshmallow toasting and mottling his legs through his frowsty cassock by the gas fire; if his mother had not called after him an urgent plea for navy blue darning wool from the couch where she lay watching a re-run of 'Belle and Sebastien' on the television, for it was the Christmas holidays; Luke would not have found himself on the frosty road to ruin that Thursday morning.

He was in a bitter mood, he had had other plans, as he walked up the hill. A sudden sluice of soapy water foamed over his feet, soaking his shoes. An old woman washing her steps had emptied her bucket. Why were old people always doing such dumb things? He caught sight of another, in a nylon overall and a hat, wiping her clothesline with a J-cloth, and an old man rubbing at his brass letter box with a piece of dirty wadding. Luke shuddered; he had sometimes been made to clean the church candlesticks with the self same stuff and hated the way it made his hands all black and dry and the way the brass curlicues deliberately bruised his fingers as he rubbed. Behind him, he heard the old man spit. What was the point of having a gleaming letter box when you voided your rheum upon the garden path? He almost tripped over a stiff-legged dog in a plastic coat starred with sleet picking its way on cold clicking pink claws towards the post office.

'Just off to get your pension, are you?' Luke inquired.

The dog rolled a moist eye and nudged open the shop door just as Luke reached for the handle, so that he lunged through the door into the back of the last person in the queue, almost setting it falling like a line of dominoes.

The post office had once been a grocer's, and a redundant bacon-slicer, huge and red and silver, seeming to threaten the wintry rumps of the customers stood by the wooden counter that still ran the length of the shop, up to the grille at the far end. Serrated orange and yellow garlands shivered in the haze of warm air from the paraffin heater above shelves stacked with packets of little toys, cardboard jigsaw puzzles, friable cars, kits for making necklaces and bracelets, dollies' vanity sets, that hinted of Christmas mornings strewn with broken plastic and tears, jammed up among the jampot covers, paper cake cases, biros, rubber bands, rubbers and ruled writing paper. Luke glared at a thriving poinsettia whose garish bracts were reproduced on a million Christmas cards. He shifted his weight from one foot to the other on the puddled floor and, like a blow to the chest, realised that there were in fact two queues, one for the post office, and one for other purchases, and that he was in the wrong one. There was nothing to be done, he was firmly wedged. The queues shuffled along, a two-headed monster studded with protuberances of sticks and umbrellas heaving its scales painfully through the mud. A wicker basket on wheels pressed into his calves as he moved to let pass a mother with a baby in a sling, whose doleful grizzling, although painful to the ear, was entirely understandable. Luke felt like joining in. As he drew nearer to the grille he realised why progress was so slow.

'– And I've brought Mrs Smith's book too. She's a bit poorly today, poor old leg's playing her up.'

'This weather doesn't help.'

'I'll say. And two telephone stamps if you please, and one, no, better make that two, television stamps and eleven thirteen and a halves. Do you mind having one of these nasty little coins?'

'It's all money!'

'Ha ha ha. Thank you very much. Have a happy Christmas.'

'And the same to you. Good morning, Mr Johnson, and how's Mr Johnson this morning?'

'Oh, not so bad, mustn't grumble.'

'That's the spirit.' The postmistress dropped her voice. 'And how's Mrs Johnson? Any improvement?'

A shake of the head.

'Fifty-five, sixty, sixty-five, seventy and five makes seventy-five. Don't spend it all at once.'

'Thank you kindly, madam. The compliments of the season to you.'

'And to you. Remember me to Mrs J, if she, you know . . .'

As the old man stumped past brushing the wing of a huge tweed overcoat against him Luke was amazed at the huge wads of notes that were being clawed into mothy wallets and handbags.

'Forty-one, forty-two –'

'Can't look after herself properly, and of course it makes more work for me, not that I mind –'

'Of course it does, and twenty makes a pound . . .'

'And I'm under the doctor myself. Take it easy, he says, I wish I could, Doctor, I said . . .'

'You know you can have two weeks' today . . .'

'I'd only spend it –'

'. . . And nineteen second-class stamps . . .'

'. . . I've brought Mr Peale's book – only I expect he's forgotten to sign it . . .'

'. . . Merry Christmas . . .'

'. . . Spread to the other lung . . .'

'. . . Ninety-nine, one hundred . . .'

'. . . And these three for Rhodesia, if you please . . .'

Now Luke was close enough to see the subpostmistress who was so tiny that she must have placed her chair on several telephone directories in order to see over the counter, rolling her eyes ceilingwards as if to indicate that she had a houseful of bedridden up there if she only cared to mention it. Of course few chose to take two weeks' allowance today, being eager not to pass up the chance of another sojourn in this ante-chamber of Death.

All that money. There must be thousands of pounds behind the counter.

It seemed that the customers were vying with each other in their seasonal wishes to the subpostmistress; some of their efforts were worthy of the cards that Luke was now studying, but there would be no mice in Santa Claus caps hiccuping cutely beside brandy glasses ballooning like their plum-pudding-stuffed stomachs, no be-muffed and bonneted ladies and top-hatted gents carolling round a lantern in the snow, no winking owl hanging its stocking from a branch in any of their gardens. In a week or two they would all be back inquiring of each other if they had had a nice Christmas.

'Very nice, thank you,' they would reply, and then add, 'Quiet . . .'

'What a tragic farce,' Luke thought, thrusting his hands deep in boredom and despair into the pockets of his Oxfam overcoat. He remembered that he was in the wrong queue.

'May you have a happy and blessed Christmas,' a woman was saying as she gathered up her muddle of Giros and stamps and pension books. Luke picked from the shelf a gun. He took a little green cardboard box of caps. He rolled the caps into the gun and fastened the safety catch.

'. . . And a happy New Year.'

Luke leaped on to the chair which had just been vacated, waved the gun and shouted.

'This is a stick-up! Everybody lie on the floor!'

The complete silence was broken by a babbling, a terrified dribble of words from an old lady's lips.

'I said, everybody lie on the floor. You' – he jabbed the gun towards the subpostmistress – 'hand over the money.' He fired into the air, the cap failed to explode. Then an ancient grabbed the back of the chair and shook it; Luke wobbled for a moment and fell; an oldie had him in an arm lock, an umbrella was jabbed into his stomach, that damned dog was at his throat, the subpostmistress worrying at his knees and someone jammed a shopping basket over his head. A balloon belched discreetly.

Through the shameful wicker he saw a policewoman's black legs and heard her radio for assistance. Someone kicked him as he was led out through a tunnel of boos and hisses and he had to sit in the police car with the basket on his head.

'It was only a joke. Just a joke,' he kept repeating after he had been charged and a constable had filed through the handle of the basket.

'I hope you find that funny then,' said the policewoman as she struck him across the face.

'I felt sorry for them,' he tried to explain to his mother, rattling the locked bathroom door. From the kitchen came the dread familiar rasp of the top of a bottle of whisky.

Now Baskethead, the scourge of the sub-post office, slept uneasily through the day in Cherry Slattery's bed. From time to time he woke for a few seconds and then let himself sink back into the unaccustomed softness of the sheets. The sere fibres of the clean but grey pillowcase parted under his head and in his restlessness he stuck his face into the gap. He dreamed that someone was twisting a wet towel round his neck. He woke in a sweat to find that someone had placed a cup of tea beside the bed. Although the tea was cold and the cup cracked, this sweet act of domesticity comforted him so that he fell at once into a peaceful sleep.

TWO

*T*HE Reverend Ichabod Ribbons was in his dank study, nodding over a copy of *Old Pybus*. The mingled breaths of the mildewed leather volumes that lined his walls and of half a dozen pipes on the rack on his desk and of the small briar between his teeth gave the room a heavy air, which was not lightened by the fingers of an old yew tree beckoning at the window, as if to lure him into the graveyard. His stomach spoke of too many years of rhubarb crumble and custard; ash fell from his pipe on to his yellow pullover, so pitted with tiny burns and black specks that it might have been a ravelled overdone omelette. From time to time a page broke off in his hand.

A cloud of bubbles passed his window unnoticed, as he nodded, sucked and chewed, but the iridescent cluster floated over a dark corner of the churchyard as the curate trickled a handful of earth and stones on to a coffin, and brought comfort to the little group of mourners, who mistook it for a sign.

Ichabod Ribbons rubbed irritably at his ear; the voice of old Boxall the gravedigger singing under his window made it impossible for him to concentrate. He let fall his book and wandered outside, almost tripping over a young girl crouched by a tombstone. She seized his hand; her tears dripped on to his fingers. He pulled them away and wiped them on his jacket. 'I expect you're looking for Richard Ruggles,' he said, looking round desperately for his curate, but the young fool was gossiping with some people at the lychgate.

'Oh Vicar, I – I've lost my – my . . . I've lost my . . .'

'Have you tried the Parish Office?' he interrupted testily. 'They've got all sorts of lost property there – gloves, umbrellas . . .'

She dashed into the shrubbery with a sob. What a big girl to be making such a fuss about losing something.

Old Boxall's dirge grew nearer and the Vicar pulled a breviary from his pocket and, under its cover, fell to examining a bead of amber resin sparkling in the fissure of a tree trunk as Boxall passed with a wheelbarrow of weeds. Two thoughts struggled weakly in his brain: that possibly neither of the things which a distraught girl might have lost could be found in the Parish Office, and that the drop of resin looked like golden syrup. He wondered if there was any hope of gypsy tart for pudding and set off for the kitchen in search of Sister Mildred, self-designated Deaconess, and housekeeper.

The plumbing groaned and sweated great rusty drops in its efforts to pump yet more hot water up to the bathroom of St Elmo's Vicarage. The bath braced its iron legs and splayed its lion's feet as a fresh cascade gushed on to the airy pyramid of bubbles, and the less insubstantial form of Mrs Ribbons. A little teapot stood on the bath's edge; a grapefruit rind, an eggshell in a rosy eggcup rimmed with gold, and an empty coffee cup lolled on a tray on the floor beside a soggy copy of the morning's *Times*.

After a life of disappointments, the latest being the downfall of her only son, Luke, she had taken to her bath; choosing an ambience of water and steam, where the only peril was the failure of the boiler. Now, while threading the chain of little silver balls round the toes of one deft foot and pulling up the plug enough to release a gallon or two of cooling water and bubbles, and turning the hot tap with the others, she poured herself a cup of tea and lay back with closed eyes, pillowed on porcelain, to drink it and think about nothing at all. From far below, she caught the strain of Boxall's dirge:

> 'My hide I'll to the huntsman give,
> My shoes I'll throw away . . .'

and kicked the hot tap harder to drown it.

When the Young Wives' Club, the Mothers' Union, the Altar Flowers Rota had all vanished down the plughole, Sister Mildred had told inquirers that Mrs Ribbons was suffering from a nervous complaint and must have complete rest. A caller at the Vicarage, passing the kitchen window and catching sight of the bloody forearms of the Deaconess cranking away at the old iron mincer, might have fancied that she had disposed of the Vicaress; but in fact theirs was a symbiotic relationship; Sister Mildred regarded climbing the stairs with trays of light refreshments and bath essences a small price to pay for the control of the Vicarage and its incumbent, and so, several times a day, her voice could be heard across the tombstones urging Boxall to come and stoke the boiler. The Vicar, once he had accustomed himself to using the small cloakroom in the lobby, had secret cause to be grateful for the transfer of power; Sister Mildred's cooking was infinitely superior to that of his wife, whom he had long suspected of incorporating the crumbling masonry of the church in her pastry.

When the Vicar came into the kitchen, the Deaconess was not there. He poured himself a cup of cooking sherry and broke off a lump of yellow cheese.

'They are not long, the days of port and Stilton,' he murmured as he nibbled. Then he caught sight of a letter on the table and opened it.

Dear Vicar,

I am not a religious man, but I do draw the line at the representation of the Holy Ghost by the inside of a toilet roll . . .

'Damn you, Ruggles!' he said, throwing it in the bin.

THREE

*W*HEN Luke stepped out on to the little balcony that opened off his new room, and overlooked Redhill's red-light district, the scent of the white trumpet-shaped blossom, whose fleshy stems and heart-shaped leaves threatened the frail stonework, was turning dusty day into fragrant evening. Two policewomen strolled hand in hand in the street below. One reached up tenderly to scoop a caterpillar or blossom from her companion's cap. Now spicy smells were mingling with blossom and Luke at once became very hungry. He had slept all day. Somewhat nervously, he sought the Slatterys' bath-room, pushing doors with a diffident finger until he found the right one. He peeked in the bathroom cabinet, and examined the writhing heap of clothes on the floor of the airing cupboard.

Showered, shimmering in a clean shirt, he entered the kitchen with his empty cup to confront the Slatterys. A greeting died on his lips. The room was empty. Then Tiffany, in pink and white frills, skated past him on white boots with pink wheels. 'Hi,' she said, snatching a majorette's baton from the table, 'bye,' and was gone. Silence drifted like pollen when a butterfly has left a flower. For a moment he almost wished himself back in the dining-room of Stillwood Hall, then before loneliness rushed like sea into a cave or the sound of the sea in a shell he went out through the unfamiliar hall, setting the chandelier clashing its dusty lustres with his hand, leaving a prismatic jangle behind him in the empty house.

A broken cone and a smear of ice-cream on the pavement gave it for a moment the air of a promenade when the visitors have left the beach and the colonnaded houses that lined the street enhanced the marine aspect; indeed the house next to the Slatterys' bore a 'Bed and Breakfast' sign and an old mattress and a heap of eggshells and tealeaves in the front garden gave credence to its claim. To the north of him was London, where no doubt people were passing the cocktail hour in dalliance and adventure and *crimes passionnels*, and to the south Brighton's palaces of pleasure glittered beside the sea. Perhaps it was the other way round; his geography had never been good, he reflected, as he set out to find what fun this town in the middle of nowhere had to offer. As he walked he perceived that Redhill was in essence a car park, or a series of car parks strung together with links of smouldering rubble and ragwort, buddleia and willowherb. An empty supermarket trolley skated dreamily across the asphalt towards him. He dodged it and walked on, led by hunger to a chip shop near the station. Boys and girls in gangs and twos and threes wandered past as he stood on the pavement eating his chips; he was the only one alone. He half hoped to see Cherry Slattery but knew that she would not deign to acknowledge him. The girls and boys, species Casual or Whammer, were streaming towards a bleak building, a converted cinema, uncharacteristically unlovely, of the thirties, with the name 'Busby's' flashing in neon in a border of lightbulbs projecting from its black-painted and cream-tiled façade, where a bouncer in evening dress waited, arms folded, at the top of the steps to welcome or repel.

A departing diesel train hooted and left hanging in the air a floweret of smoke and a feeling of such desolation, as it plunged towards Reigate, Betchworth, Deepdene and the green interior, that Luke turned at once towards a pub that he had half noticed and headed for its unwelcoming door. As he passed a flower shop he saw a forgotten bunch of clove carnations wilting in a conical green tin vase and lifted them out and wrapped them in his chip paper which he still held in a greasy ball in his hand. He saw at once that he had chosen the most unfashionable pub in Redhill. At first he thought that it was empty, then he saw, at the far end of the bar, what appeared to be a solitary lascar slumped over a schooner of sherry, his white coat splashed with the sauces of some restaurant kitchen, mirrored almost to infinity in gloomy glass, so that behind him massed sufficient lascars to staff the galleys of a whole fleet of Conradian vessels ploughing through the China Sea. Luke's nod to him was scorned. A small Siamese cat who walked along the bar was more friendly: Cio-Cio-San, Luke read on the disc on his collar, and the Surrey Puma on the obverse. The landlord, who was now hulking unenthusiastically towards Luke, had once sung Suzuki in a Church Lads production; now the obi he had worn would scarcely make a tie for his neck. He pushed a sloppy glass of beer towards Luke. The lascar put 'When a Child Is Born' by Johnny Mathis on the jukebox. Luke sipped his warm flat beer, staring at the gravy-coloured walls, the carpet simmering like stew at his feet, tables floating like greasy dumplings, and was almost tempted to darken the forbidden door of St Elmo's Vicarage. His mother: hadn't she sometimes been kind to him? Although his letter to her from Stillwood Hall HM Borstal telling her of his impending release had been returned in a soggy state which suggested that she had either wept long and bitterly over it or dropped it in the bath. He decided to spend the last of his money on another beer. When he sat down with it at a little glass-topped table he realised that the first one had gone to his head. He thought that he should be planning his future but he couldn't see that he had one and then he fell to studying a foursome that had come in undetected and were obviously discussing, in subdued tones, their chances in the Final of the Ugliest Person in the World Contest. His money would have been on the one with the beard which broke in half-hearted orange burrs from the insides of his ears, gained confidence as it rolled down his purple cheeks, merged with twin rivulets from his nose, circled his moist red lips, and fell in full triumphant flood on to the breast of his white T-shirt, but it was a close-run thing. Eventually Luke went into the Gents. He was washing his hands when the bearded man came in. Luke stood staring at him.

'What's up with you?'

'I suppose there's no point in shaving it off now,' Luke replied pleasantly. 'I mean, people would always know that you were capable of such a beard, that it was lurking in your nose and chin, ready to spring out . . .'

A bunch of gingery knuckles striking his own chin knocked Luke's head back against the graffiti on the wall behind him. He slid to the floor.

Meanwhile, at her tea break, instead of adjourning to the tiny staff room, Pearl Slattery hung up her cap and overall and walked off the assembly line into the hot street. She felt a thin sheen of sweat on her face and her shoes slid about on her feet as she walked the short distance to the Surrey Puma. She felt slighted and snubbed; she had been assigned to the least popular line, toasted coconut caramels, and had been forced to stand in a blizzard of charred desiccated coconut watching a young girl, who had started only that night, who had hitched her overall to mini length over a belt, twirling exquisite rosettes on to the choicest chocolates. Not that any of the products of Snashfold's Sweet Factory was really particularly choice; the chocolate was poor and soon developed a white bloom. The woman standing next to her had stepped heavily on her toe and tears sprang to her eyes. Above the music from the radio, which played continuously, she heard snatches of conversation concerning new kitchen units. She blinked away an image of her own sponge mop which was losing its head and left gobbets of wet grey honeycomb on the kitchen floor. She supposed that she would always be the sort of person who, while others discussed ceramic hobs, would be grubbing about in the bottom of a handbag for a half-pence to make up the price of a packet of cigarettes. And now there was this extra boy to contend with. Not for the first time, she cursed Jack Slattery.

Pearl had grown up in a black tarred shack at the side of the railway line where her father was level-crossing keeper. Her mother had, one day, packed a cardboard suitcase and flagged down the Sevenoaks train and never been seen again. Pearl and her two sisters, Violet and Belda, had run about barefoot, scratching with the chickens in the dust, pelting passing trains with coal, and smoking rolled-up newspaper. Now Violet ran a small casino in Rhyl and Belda was a nun. She sometimes sent Holy Bookmarks at Christmas. Pearl would have to decide whether to go back to work. Four people pushed past her as she went into the pub; she inhaled them; a cocktail of cosmetics, sweat and beer, and wrinkled her nose.

'Large gin and slimline, Malcolm,' she said to the barman. 'Easy on the tonic, I'm trying to cut down on my fluid intake,' she added as he started to pour it in. She pulled a paper napkin from a glass on the bar and pleated it. Luke, emerging from the Gents, saw her there, swaying gently on her stool, one elbow propped on the bar, fanning herself with a white paper fan.

'These are for you,' he said, coming up to her and thrusting the carnations at her. She plunged her face into the petals, wondering for a moment who he was.

'Mmm, gorgeous. A bit vinegary, but gorgeous. You shouldn't have . . .'

'It's all right, no one saw me,' he almost replied as he sat down beside her.

'What have you done to your face?'

'I was attacked in the Gents.'

'Oh dear. What are you drinking?'

Luke sipped his beer in a slight sulk that she did not show more concern, demand to know who had done it, soothe his injuries with tender fingers. Pearl was disinclined to talk and soon a procession of Dolly Parton numbers on the jukebox added to her melancholy and would have made speech inaudible. The pain in Luke's jaw dissolved into a not unpleasant glow and he fingered a small lump on the back of his head. The lascar left and two more glasses appeared in front of them. Luke fell into a daze; he could hear speech around him but couldn't translate it; he saw the words as black ideographs painted on the smoky air. He became aware of Pearl shaking his arm.

'What?'

'I said, I suppose there's not much point in going back to work now. We'd better get back, Tiffany will be home.'

She stood up and Luke got up too, touched by her assumption that they would leave together. He stumbled on the step.

'Come on, you'd better take my arm.'

Her hair looked rich and mineral, shining in hennaed copper wires in the green light from a street lamp, and grazed his face in a rough cloud of vanilla as they crossed the road. He slurred his footsteps and sagged against her, pretending to be drunker than he was so that he could lurch along in the intoxication of her hair. The night drained the gaudy colours from her dress; he could faintly feel her ribs under soft flesh as they walked and his heart beating in his own ribs. But when they staggered through the front door he was shot from her arm by the sound of gunfire. Tiffany was lying on the sofa reading a comic, while the television blazed away unregarded, shuffling an empty crisp bag on the carpet with her bare foot.

'Bed, Tiff.'

The child broke into a prolonged whine, and Luke sublimated an impulse to gag her with one of the crisp packets – he felt that it might not endear him to her mother – by sweeping a pile of crumbs under the edge of the rug. Tiffany embarked on a series of seemingly pointless anecdotes about her day while Luke, excluded, sat and sulked. At last she departed. 'I don't want Cherry to sleep in my room,' she whined, staring at Luke.

'I'll come and tuck you up in a minute,' said Pearl picking up a mail–order catalogue.

'Will you come and tuck me up?' asked Luke.

'Funny, I don't remember ordering this book,' she replied. 'Must've been one of the kids.'

Luke moved to the arm of her chair.

'So many things no one could possibly want,' she sighed.

Pages of rings, watches, duvets, kitchen equipment, tools, suitcases, video games flicked through her fingers. Luke leaned closer. He saw a faint wash of freckles on her skin above the low neckline of her dress. He lowered his head on to her shoulder and put out a finger to trace the chain round her neck. She pushed him away.

'Time for bed, I think.'

'Just what I was thinking.'

Pearl stood up. Luke caught her hand and as she pulled away her ring grazed his lip. The front door slammed and there was the sound of many heavy boots in the hall.

'I'm bleeding,' he accused.

'Bleeding nuisance,' he thought he heard from her head, bowed again over the catalogue, as he backed out of the room. He stood for a few moments in the doorway willing her to look up, then had to turn towards the stairs. Half-way up, he stopped, grasping the banister, and looked through the open kitchen door. Sean and half a dozen friends were slumped round the room, eating toast. He threw himself on Cherry's bed and fell asleep fully clothed among the charred crusts of his first day.

FOUR

THE house where Luke, the young Slatterys, and perhaps one or two extras, for it was always likely that there was someone in a sleeping bag on the floor of one of the children's rooms or in one of their beds, and, at last, Pearl in her chaste double bed, slept, had been built in 1907 and had been bought by the Slatterys in a brief flowering of affluence, with a view to doing it up. Slatterys, however, did not do things up, and the house, in 1982, remained unchanged except by time. There was a set of bells in a glass case on the kitchen wall and a bell-push in each room, except in the one which had been the maid's room and where Pearl now lay, her cheek pillowed on and stuck to a creased page of an Erle Stanley Gardner; she was dreaming that she had fallen asleep with the light on and that she was getting up to switch it off. The bulb made a small tinkling explosion as the filament died and she lay bathed in sodium, from a street lamp strained through the thin curtains like yellow juice through muslin. A cat oozed over the top of the open window, jumped on to the bed and bit her face gently. When she would not wake he amused himself by butting a pair of earrings off the dressing-table.

Cherry sometimes remembered those heady days, when it

had seemed for a while that they were going to be posh, with a pang. A lady from across the road had brought them a cake on the day they moved in. She had never called again and soon after, she had moved away. A letter came asking for the return of her cake tin. The Slatterys had gone on Saturday shopping trips to Croydon, just like real people; once Tiffany had been lost in Allders' carpet department for four hours and had to be tannoyed. Soon the furniture, and then Dad, had been taken away. How Cherry sympathised with Amy when she said in that pathetic way which so touched the other girls, 'When Papa was rich . . .' A blue broken-spined copy of *Little Women* lay under her bed, under Luke. All that remained from their brief prosperity were two gold dolphins that held the toilet roll and a gold dolphin with a ring in its mouth that held the bathroom towel. There was no central heating; warmth in winter was supplied by sticks and logs gathered from the common, when anybody could be bothered, and burned in the grate of the front room; by a collection of perilous gas fires and electric fires with frayed flexes placed against the art nouveau tiles of the other fireplaces, and by lighting the oven and leaving the door open.

'Morning has bro-ken, bro-ken . . .' The notes of an inept recorder shrilled into Luke's skull and forced open his eyes. He winced at a Snoopy poster on the wall, as he swung his feet, stiff in their shoes, over the side of the bed, and was at once suffused with shame at the memory of the previous night. His stomach felt like an empty landscape under a blazing red sunrise. A smell of toast drifted under the door. The recorder faltered and stopped. He drifted round the room, wanting to go to the bathroom, but not daring to open his door. The room was papered in a fading green geometric design, like cross-sections of unripe passion fruit; above the dado, from some older day, of pineapples, cherries and grapes, borders of flaky plaster met the ceiling and converged at a creamy fly-specked rose from which was suspended a light bulb encased in a lacy, tasselled mob-cap. The whole room was really neat, he thought. An orderly shelf of schoolbooks was flanked by a prim rabbit in a frock and petticoat, and a ceramic pomander; a simple jar of cleansing cream and a coral necklace stood and lay in front of the mirror on the chipped teak dressing-table. He had the corals round his neck when the door burst open.

'Excuse me.'

Cherry, in her school uniform, headed for the bookshelf, then turned to accuse:

'There's a copy of *Waiting for Godot* missing from this shelf. Have you taken it?'

'Why should I?'

'Why indeed. It's not in the bed, is it?'

'I don't know.' He couldn't say that he had spent the night fully dressed on its surface. Cherry was pulling at the covers, whipping up an electric storm of sheet in the stifling room. The ancient pillowcase tore in two as she flung herself across the bed to look under it.

'I can't find the bloody thing. It's too hot. I hate the summer!' She pummelled the bed. 'And the winter. And the autumn. And the spring. Why don't you say something, instead of standing there sweating?'

'I never sweat,' replied Luke hotly, running a finger across his forehead. She slammed out of the room. Luke was left staring at a long cone of green light streaming through a diamond of stained glass, set in the window, which struck the edge of the bookshelf and hit the mirror, almost turning him into a negative of himself, complete with coral beads.

When at last he dared go downstairs hoping that the kids would have gone, he found Pearl in a pink quilted dressing-gown with tinselly piping on the collar, pockets, and hem; a loop of fraying gold made bids to lasso the heel of her slipper as she moved about the kitchen, and she was not alone. He saw that his carnations were already tinged with brown; his heart was beating painfully. A man on the little portable television was instructing viewers in the art of cooking offal.

'I love hearts,' he said. 'I love young hearts and I love plump hearts.'

'Want some toast?' asked Pearl.

'No, thank you, I mean, yes, please,' he said miserably. Tiffany was standing on the kitchen stool arranging her hair in the mirror.

'Do you think my hair looks better like this', she said, 'or like this?'

He considered. 'No,' he replied. 'Isn't Tiffany going to school?' he asked Pearl.

'I think that if you force children to go to school when they don't want to, it only encourages truancy, don't you?'

He thought that he agreed with the logic as he chewed his cold toast, willing Tiffany to go away.

'Are you going to work today?'

'Not till this evening.'

That meant that he had all day in which to speak. Pearl turned from the sink with a milk bottle full of rainbows.

'You could have a cup of tea, if there was a cup. Tiffany, go round all the bedrooms and collect all the cups and mugs and glasses . . .'

'Why can't he?'

'Do as you're told.'

With many complaints about the unfairness of life, she grumbled her way slowly out of the kitchen. Luke went and lounged against the sink.

'I'm sorry about last night,' he muttered.

'What for?'

'Well, you know . . .'

'Don't be so silly – you just had a bit too much to drink, that's all.'

'I –'

'Come on, out of the way!' she slapped at him. Her hand glanced off his arm.

'Ouch!'

He wandered in a daze into the garden and threw himself down on the tussocky grass. The slap burned like a star: he could feel each finger pulsating on his skin. He was smitten; literally, metaphorically, irrevocably.

25

Bees throbbed in the lavender. The marigolds were clotted with blackfly which clung to the stems while ants walked up and down on them. He wondered if the ants were eating the blackfly. Everything that grew there was a survivor from the past, or had seeded itself from other gardens. The fence was hung with convolvulus and ropes of roses whose leaves were blurred with silvery blight; hollyhocks like temple bells swayed in a grassy bed; the irises were in rags. Luke reached out and popped a white bell out of its green socket and rolled it between his fingers into a slimy brown ball. The bindweed exuded the rank scent of boredom, of long hot futile childhood days in the Vicarage garden.

'Fancy doing that at your age!'

The scornful face of Tiffany expelled the words through chocolatey lips. Her mother's fingers still glowed on his arm; he supposed he ought to love the daughter.

'Hi,' he said pleasantly. 'What are you doing?'

'What is there to do?' She flung herself on her back, arms and legs sprawling starwise from T-shirt and shorts. From an open window came the sound of 'It might as well rain until September'.

'What's your mum doing?'

'She's gone out. You've got to keep an eye on me.'

'Oh.' He felt, absurdly, betrayed.

Through a broken slat in the fence he could see two tortoises. The grass was so dry and brown that it looked as though a cigarette butt could turn all of Redhill into an immense conflagration. Twists of smoke rose from what had once been a street. Half a house stood starkly against the blue sky; torn layers of faded patterns like papier mâché stuck to its jagged walls, and half-way up a sink fit now only for rinsing rain and clouds, made a pathetic memorial to the generations which had lived there.

'I don't suppose you want to come to collect some stuff from my house with me?'

'Where is it?'

'Near Purley.'

'It's too hot. Why don't you live there then?'

Luke didn't answer. He wandered into the house. Sean and two girls were watching 'Playschool'.

'It's not fair, Big Ted gets all the best jobs,' one of them was saying as Luke went in.

'Yeah, it's never Hamble, is it?'

'And it's the bloody arched window again. Why can't it ever be the square or round window?'

'Anyone want to come to Purley?' Luke asked hopefully.

'Nah, we're going down Reigate.'

Much to his surprise, when Cherry came home, she had a free afternoon, she agreed to go with him.

'There's one small problem,' he warned her.

'I'll get the fares,' she said resignedly. 'Where's the bus timetable, Tiff?'

'Goblin was eating it. It's under the fridge.'

Goblin was not the Slatterys' cat. He sometimes came for meals, and was now eating a bit of meat from a messy milky bowl on the floor.

'Is Goblin Jewish?' asked Luke.

'Dunno, why?'

'He's always breaking the food laws.'

'He used to be a rabbi,' said Sean, 'but they chucked him out for bad behaviour.'

'What did he do?'

'He was accused of eating two members of the congregation, two very orthodox mice. They couldn't prove anything, but two tails were found in the Ark . . .'

'Poor Goblin,' Tiffany scooped him up and held him, hind legs dangling. 'You didn't, did you?'

'If we go now we can get the 414,' said Cherry.

On the bus Luke tried to prepare her a bit.

'My father . . .' he began.

'What about him?'

'He's a bit, well, religious. In fact he's a vicar,' he mumbled.

'Well, somebody's got to be, I suppose,' she said kindly.

27

Luke stared out of the window. A street sign said 'Stoats Nest Lane'.

The fried egg sandwich he had had for lunch sat heavily on him.

'What's your mum like?'

'She's all right. We probably won't see her – she might be in the bath or something.'

'I don't think the driver believed we were halves, do you?'

'Couldn't prove it though, could he?'

'Why do we have to climb over the wall?' Cherry complained. 'My skirt's too tight. Why can't we go in the front way?'

To Luke's disgust they almost tumbled into the arms of Rick Ruggles, the Curate, who was doing a rubbing of an old gravestone; skulls and bones and angels' wings.

'Greetings,' he said hoarsely, attempting nonchalance.

'Why are you whispering?' said Luke.

'I've lost my voice.'

'Perhaps it's Nature's way of telling you to shut up,' suggested Luke.

'Ha, ha, ha,' laughed Ruggles without conviction.

'Have you tried filling an old sock with boiled manure and tying it round your neck?'

'No,' he replied doubtfully. 'Does it work?'

'No, but it's very unpleasant.'

'Don't be so rude!' Cherry tugged at Luke's arm. Rick Ruggles smiled at her. Luke saw she was smiling back. He had to get her away before it was too late.

'I don't think we've seen you here before?'

Ruggles was twinkling at Cherry.

'No.'

'Come on, Cherry,' Luke pulled her arm. She shrugged off his hand.

'You go on. I'll wait for you here.'

'Cherry, you don't realise that you are in grave danger . . .'

Then he saw something large and black and dusty parting the branches of two intertwined yew trees and ran for the house before his father saw him. The kitchen door was open; he collided with the Deaconess and left her sitting on the floor in a confusion of sweetbreads and breadcrumbs as he bolted up the stairs. Half-way up on a little landing, a grandfather clock tottered and almost fell as he passed. A broken stair-rod caught his foot on the top step, and he sprawled on the familiar musty cracked linoleum, hearing a gurgling sound at the end of the passage. He picked himself up and walked past bedroom doors to the bathroom.

'Mother?' he tapped on the door.

There was an answering waterfall from within.

'Mother!' he knocked louder. The waterfall doubled in volume as the second tap was turned on. He stood for a few moments picking a splinter of linoleum out of his knee, wondering what she was thinking of as she lay in that steamy Niagara.

He gave the door an angry kick which made an excuse for tears to spring to his eyes.

'There's a toothbrush of mine in there!' he shouted. 'And a duck.'

As he stuffed his clothes into his rucksack he pictured that duck's red and yellow head poking out of his Christmas stocking; that was the year they had forgotten to buy him any presents and the only shop open late on Christmas Eve was the emergency chemist. His stocking had bulged with soap and bath cubes of violet-scented chalk, a packet of Disprin, a family size bottle of disinfectant, a pretty hair net hung with tiny glass beads, which he had rather liked but puzzled over, a pair of Dr Scholl's insoles, two kinds of toothpaste and an economy size jar of Vaseline. They had drawn the line at razor blades.

'Luke!' His father's voice roared up the stairs. He grabbed a piggy-bank from the dressing-table and was half-way down a perilous swag of ivy when the black cassock burst into the room. The Reverend Ribbons grabbed handfuls of ivy, trying to haul Luke back through the window but his feet touched ground and, with painful ankles, he ran for the wall.

'Ah well,' said the Vicar aloud and picking up a dusty copy of *My Guy* sank down on the bed to peruse a page of Tasty Fellas.

'A most unattractive lot,' he mused. Surely there was some sort of tinted cream they could apply to disguise their spots? A small piece of blood-stained tissue adhering to his chin fluttered in the hot draught from the open window.

'Luke, wait!' Luke turned and saw Cherry, Rick Ruggles beside her, waving. 'I've got the bus tickets!' she shouted so he had to walk back to join them.

'Wouldn't it have been easier and quicker to have caught the train?' Ruggles was asking.

'There is no quick and easy way to the Purley Gates, Rick,' Luke told him.

'Many a true word spoken in jest, old son.' Ruggles's eyes became grave. 'Look, why don't you give Taskforce another chance? You've got a lot to offer, you know . . .'

'Taskforce?' said Cherry.

'It's our youth group. Why don't you come along on Sunday?'

'I, well, I live in Redhill . . .'

'*Pas de problème*, several of our young folk come from your neck of the woods. Give me your number and I'll see what I can fix up, and try to persuade this young man to come with you.'

'Our telephone's been – out of order.'

'Well, give me your address, I'll drop you a line, or call when I'm passing.'

'Thank you, and about our talk – well, thanks, I'll think about what you said.'

'Oh God,' said Luke.

'I should have known it would be a mistake to take you,' grumbled Luke on the bus.

'What?' She turned on him a smile he knew too well, eyes radiant and blank, reflecting Ruggles back at him.

'Why is that road called Stoats Nest Lane?' he asked.

30

'What?'

'Oh forget it.' He pictured a nest of stoats, pale brown sinuous bodies intertwined.

'Do you know how to tell a stoat from a weasel?' he said.

'Oh yes.' She jerked herself back to reality. '"You can easily tell the stoat from the weasel by the simple fact that his tail is blacked and his figure is slightly the bigger." Enid Blyton. *The Children of Cherry Tree*, or *Willow Farm*.'

'At least we share a common culture,' said Luke, and the rest of the journey passed in silence.

They arrived home just as a friend of Tiffany's, who had been to tea, was being collected by her mother, Helen Headley-Jones, a tallish woman known to the Slatterys as the Weasel. Luke of course did not yet know this, so was unable to check if she had a tail. She always gave the impression of standing on her hind legs, and carried a small head on a long neck at an indignant angle, poised to nip. She was the sort of person who would stride into a railway compartment and fling open the window without consulting the people who were sitting there. Prematurely grey hair sprung vigorously from her round forehead above her perpetually inquiring expression; either her hair was too old for her face, or her youthful skin too fresh for her hair. She looked somehow incomplete.

'Mum,' the little friend was saying, 'we had real spaghetti for tea. And proper bread. Why can't we have proper bread?'

'Do you bake all your own bread?' the Weasel asked Pearl, slightly incredulously. 'Of course I do a batch myself from time to time, but I simply don't have . . .'

She stopped as she caught sight of the Mother's Pride wrapper on the table and an empty Heinz tin laughing at her with its jagged lid.

'Well, what do you say, Ruth?'

'Thank you for having me. Mummy, why can't we have Coco Pops for pudding?'

'I'm sorry she's a bit of a mess,' apologised Pearl, surveying

31

the face of the little guest, daubed pink and blue like a mandrill. 'They were playing with my old make-up.'

'It's ridiculous,' said Sean, 'when I was their age I was still playing with dolls. Mum, what did happen to my twin dolls' pram?'

'Come along, Ruth, we'll be late for Brownies. And where are your sandals? I don't know what Brown Owl would have to say to Mrs Slattery's old shoes!'

'She'd say, "Hello Mrs Slattery's old shoes, you're too old for Brownies, you'll have to go up to Guides",' said Sean, running his finger round the empty spaghetti tin and licking it.

'Sean!' Pearl caught him a slap round the head; she was rather peeved as the shoes were, in fact, in constant use. Luke wished that he had said it, as the lucky devil grinned and rubbed his stubble.

'Are you coming to the Parents' Evening on Monday?' the Weasel was asking Pearl.

'I'm not sure.'

'Would you like a lift, or will Mr Slattery be taking you? Is he back from his business trip?' she asked with heavy delicacy.

'I . . .'

Pearl was left gulping air as Weasel and young exited, past the disconnected telephone.

'Well, give me a ring if you'd like a lift, or I can pop in on my way . . .'

'What Parents' Evening?' Pearl turned on Tiffany as soon as they had gone.

'How should I know?' Tiffany shrugged.

'You always have to show me up, don't you?'

'Stupid little skiver,' said Sean. 'If you ever went to school you'd know these things.'

'Hark who's talking.'

'Well, it's not *my* fault Daddy's in prison,' said Tiffany primly and was pursued from the kitchen by Sean and Pearl.

'This family's so bloody un-Christian,' complained Cherry, switching on the television. 'D'you want some toast, Luke?'

32

Luke dug the piggy-bank out of his rucksack and unscrewed its snout.

'This is towards my keep,' he said to Pearl, who had returned, shaking the pig over his outstretched hand.

'Well, it's the thought that counts,' she replied, pocketing the fourteen and a half pence.

'Somebody's been at it,' he muttered, blushing savagely. 'That thieving Deaconess . . . I'll go to the Job Centre tomorrow, or sign on.'

'It's Saturday,' Sean pointed out.

'Well, Monday then,' he said with some relief.

'Well, I must be off to work.' Pearl smoothed down her skirt, patterned with huge roses. 'Does this skirt make me look like a three-piece suite?'

'You couldn't look like a three-piece suite,' said Luke at once, 'only a sofa, perhaps, or a chair.'

'Thanks a lot!'

'I didn't mean . . .' He could see she was hurt. 'I only meant . . .'

'Oh forget it.' She turned to the sideboard. 'Is there any of that wine left, Sean?'

'Nah.'

'"O for a beaker full of the warm South,"' she sighed, going out. It was one of the few things she had retained from her days at Tonbridge Girls' Grammar School, where she could not help but notice that she was the only girl who wore wellies all through the summer; the family budget did not run to the indoor and outdoor shoes demanded.

Luke flung himself on his bed and lay staring miserably at the paper passion fruit, wishing and wishing he had not hurt her.

'Listen, Bigmouth.' Sean appeared in the doorway. 'Now you've gone and put Mum in a mood. I was going to ask her to lend me some money. Got any more in that pig of yours?'

Luke shook his head.

'Got any fags then?'

'No, sorry.'

'Can I borrow this T-shirt? Just for tonight?'

'OK.'

Sean pulled off his shirt and put on Luke's T-shirt and posed in front of the mirror.

'D'you think it makes my neck look kind of vulnerable? Don't mind if I rip the sleeves out, do you? Ta.'

He was gone. Luke's next visitor was Cherry. She knocked on his door and entered at once and sat down heavily on the end of the bed.

'It's not fair.'

'What isn't?'

'We've been blacklisted at the library and I really need some books for study.'

'Couldn't you go to a different library?'

'Blacklisted throughout the county. I don't suppose . . . ?'

'You mean, I could join and get your books? I don't mind.'

'Oh would you?' she cried. 'Great!'

Perhaps it would put him in Pearl's good books.

'Life's so difficult, isn't it?' she said. 'My mother thinks UCCA is some sort of house plant.'

FIVE

SATURDAY night in Redhill; from Busby's the distant sound of breaking glass, a short scream, a police siren. Through the window, an aquarelle under glass, the delicate greenish iron tracery of a gas holder rose against the green sky above Hooley Lane. Luke stood staring at it, thinking of nothing, aware of a slight heaviness in his chest, which had been there since he had stood outside the bathroom door in the Vicarage, but unaware of its cause. He had no desire to seek out his friends; he thought of them as his former friends. His life hitherto was like a set of stills, fading to sepia, from an old movie which he had no desire to watch again. The Slatterys had become his reality, and of them, chiefly Pearl. Her husband, Jack, he had known for only a few days, in the prison to which he had been remanded before being transferred to Stillwood Hall. The first sharp shock of his short sentence had been the severing of the little pigtail which had hung down the back of his neck. Then he had fallen under the protection of a youth named Slasher McCrow with a Union Jack tattooed on his scalp and life had not been too bad, for him at least. Others were much less fortunate. This was typical of Luke; on his first day at school he had cried at dinner time and thereafter the headmaster had eaten his greens for him.

He went down to the kitchen. Pearl was not there. Tiffany, he knew, was spending the night with a friend. He picked up and rejected a toasted coconut caramel, a dingy white cube dipped in tinted sawdust, and poked at a bowl of fruit and vegetables on the table; white onions, green peppers, lemons. The onion skins were loose and papery and green shoots curved round the dish. The peppers were losing their gloss and starting to crinkle. The lemons were dry and hard. Tiny blue dots of corruption were on them all. They had been bought for their beauty by Pearl and, never intended for consumption, would end up rotting in the bin under the sink when a fresh trolley full of goodies arrived from Safeway's. Luke ran his fingers along the spines of a little shelf of cookery books: *Making the Most of Vegetables, Take a Leek, Not Just a Load of Old Lentils* . . . A faint odour of chips hung in the air. He decided to risk going to the pub to see if Pearl was there. In the hall he met Sean coming in, and Cherry going out. Behind the closed front room door a guitar wailed, a voice sobbed and died.

'Oh no.'

'God.'

The Slatterys froze, then melted in opposite directions. Luke stood staring to see what had scared them off. The man's mournful voice started on another song, soon breaking into plangent tears. Luke went to Sean's room and pushed open the door. Sean was lying on the unmade bed under a cloud of cigarette smoke; the walls were papered with hundreds of pictures and posters of David Bowie; broken glass on the floor suggested enough bad luck to last a lifetime.

'What happened? Why did you both rush off like that?'

'She's playing her Dr Hook records,' said Sean from the bed, as if that explained everything.

'So?'

'You wouldn't understand.'

Luke had to scrunch away again. He gently opened the front

36

room door and went in. Pearl was sitting on the floor with her back against the sofa, in a scattering of record sleeves, with a bottle of gin and one of tonic beside her.

'Do you mind if I join you?'

She shrugged. Pain and loss were spinning on the turntable and pouring out of the one extant speaker, muffled by the curtain because Pearl thought it ugly, disillusion and a past irrecoverable by her and unknowable to him. He thought that he might understand what Sean had meant.

'Get yourself a glass if you like,' said Pearl in a congested voice. 'You might have to finish the Nutella . . .'

In the kitchen, as he licked the last traces of Nutella from his finger, and washed the glass, Luke heard Sean's boots in the hall and the front door slam. Now he and Pearl were alone in the house. His heart was racing, he felt full of bubbles like a bottle of Coke that has been shaken; he couldn't speak when he returned and sat down near her. She poured a huge amount of gin into his glass and he added a splash of tonic, spilling only a few drops as he tripped on an ancient copy of the *Surrey Mirror* which was lying on the floor. 'Woodhatch Gay Pride Week Washout', read the headline over a picture of a lone morris dancer smoking a cigarette under a dripping umbrella. A tear splashed on to the photograph, adding a touch of verisimilitude. Luke cleared his throat.

'What's wrong?'

'Everything.'

The record had come to its end and punctuated the silence with regular clicks.

'It would take about twenty-five years to tell you,' said Pearl at last, 'and you might have other things to do with your life . . .'

'I wouldn't.'

He picked up her hand and laced his through it so that their fingers made a branched candlestick.

'Better change the record,' she said.

'What shall I put on?'

'Anything, so long as it's not cheerful.'

37

'Elvis's Golden Records Vol. 2?'

'That'll do.'

They sat without speaking while Elvis sang and Pearl cried. Luke wished he had a manly white handkerchief to offer her. He had to get a wodge of loo paper. He put his arm round her as he gave it to her and she didn't push him away; he edged closer to her, picking up her glass and putting it to her lips and then darting a little furtive kiss at her lips as he withdrew the glass. When he got up to turn over the record he caught a little smile reflected in the record player's perspex lid. He took a cigarette from the pack on the floor and lit it and took a drag, inhaling a blurred golden feeling of perfect calm and rightness; there was plenty of gin in the bottle, almost a full pack of cigarettes and endless time before them.

'You know I love you,' he said.

'Oh God, not you too,' she might have mumbled, or 'I love you too.' He was not quite sure.

'Everything will be all right,' he told her. He planted kisses up and down her arm, stopping at her wedding ring and trying to remove it with his teeth but it would not come off her finger.

'It's not just me, is it? You feel it too, don't you?' he insisted.

Her eyes rolled backwards in acquiescence or drunkenness. He dared to put his hand on her breast. The doorbell rang. She jerked away wildly, flailing a helpless hand at the bottles, the mess on the floor.

'I'll go,' said Luke savagely.

A woman stood on the doorstep, accompanied by Tiffany.

'She wasn't feeling very well,' she explained, taking Luke for Tiffany's brother, 'so I thought I'd better pop her back.'

'Thank you,' said Luke.

When the door was closed he said, 'You go upstairs and I'll get your mum.'

He hadn't reached the sitting-room when there was a gushing sound and a prolonged wail of 'Mu-um, I've been sick.'

'Quick, get the *Surrey Mirror*.' Pearl rushed out.

So the evening of passion expired in a scrumpling of news-paper and the smell of disinfectant and regurgitated chips.

Sunday morning: a pale pinkish-yellow plasmatic smell of half-cooked meat hung over the back gardens. In the Slatterys' kitchen their Sunday lunch, five tubs of pot noodles, steamed gently waiting for the family to assemble. Luke had gone into the garden to try to clear the grey cloud from his brain and had found Tiffany there unwrapping an ice lolly. He was terribly thirsty; the legacy of the gin. He glared at her, remembering how she had ruined the evening.

'Give us a bite.'

She shook her head.

'Go on, five pence for half, OK?'

She pondered, then reluctantly held it out to him. He broke it in two.

'You pig! You've taken the big half!'

'Never give a sucker an even break,' he told her as the orange ice dissolved on his tongue.

'What about my 5p?'

Then Pearl's voice was heard calling from the kitchen.

'Where's Cherry?' asked Luke as they went in.

'Church.'

'Which church?'

'I dunno. St Lemon's or summink. Some man came to get her in a car.'

Luke banged his fist on the doorpost at the thought of St Elmo's dank tentacles crawling after him and writhing into his new life. On the radio Jimmy Savile was saying that three of the artistes featured on today's show were now singing up in Heaven. After Luke had washed up, which did not take long and for which no one seemed grateful, Pearl asked if anybody would like to take a walk to Earlswood Lakes. Everybody refused but Luke, and then Pearl changed her mind and said she had a headache, so he set out miserably, alone, with no idea of where he was going.

★

39

In the Italian corner of Redstone Cemetery, sparkling granite and obsidian and heavy red ceramic roses and a displaced sheaf of carmine and scarlet flowers with green stalks as thick as rhubarb were embedded in the wet grass; a crown of rhubarb, a crown of thorns, Luke sat on a bench in the sun; beyond the green slope of the cemetery rose a dense mass of trees. People moved among the graves with watering cans and flowers and secateurs. Luke hoped that passers-by might pity the boy, solitary in his grief, who sat alone with his melancholy thoughts in that foreign corner of an English field.

'Take your feet off that seat! People have got to sit there.'

At the man's sharp voice, Luke jumped up guiltily, and face as red as the china roses, scuffed his way down the path to the gates.

When he returned he found the kitchen full of people; a tall brown man and two little black girls, and started to back out, wanting only to see Pearl alone.

'Luke, this is my son, Elvis, and these are my two grand-daughters, Grace and Gemma.'

'Pleased to meet you.' Elvis stuck out a hand.

'Hi,' said Luke faintly, as the two little girls giggled and one splattered her Coca-Cola over the table, proving beyond doubt her Slattery ancestry.

'Cup of tea?' said Pearl.

'Thank you.' He sat down. 'I didn't know you had another son.' He tried not to sound accusing as he sipped his tepid tea.

'Elvis is from my first marriage.' 'If it's any of your business,' she might as well have added, from her tone.

'Please can we get down, Nan?'

'Yes, go and find Aunty Tiffany to play with.'

They slid down with a clashing of the beads in their hair and flashing of long white socks.

'Where did you say Precious had gone?' asked Pearl.

Elvis dipped a biscuit into his tea and rolled his eyes.

'She done gone down Reigate way, visit de obeah man.'

'Don't be so silly,' snapped his mother.

40

'True, there's this Sister at the hospital keeps picking on her so she's going to put a spell on her.'

'Load of rubbish!'

'What sort of spell? D'you mean like a curse or what?' Luke forgot his animosity.

'Nothing too drastic. Just something to make her lay off. A warning, if you like.'

'Does he do other things, like potions and that?'

'I wouldn't know really. Well, I suppose I'd better get those two home. See you, Mum.' He dropped a kiss on her head.

'Who's Precious?' Luke asked when they had gone.

'Elvis's wife. She's a nurse, as you may have gathered.'

'You never told me you were a grandmother.'

'You never asked.'

Seven o'clock in the evening found Pearl in front of the television in the pleasantly melancholic miasma that 'Songs of Praise' always induced in her, singing along, in between sips from a glass of Belle Cave Rouge, in a voice that was sometimes soprano and sometimes contralto and rarely hit the note, to 'Dear Lord and Father of Mankind'. The total conviction of the congregation was somewhat unnerving, she felt as she puffed smoke towards their faces; supposing they were right? It was too scary to contemplate. Upstairs in his room Sean was unscrewing the cap of a small white bottle of Tipp-Ex thinner in preparation for a little solvent abuse before going out. Tiffany was working on a collage for school, without much enthusiasm; her last effort, an icon in rice and lentils, had been cooked and eaten.

Unknown to Cherry, who had not yet returned from Morning Service at St Elmo's, Pearl had once given her heart to Jesus, in response to a plea from a gentle Church Army Sister with whom she had fallen in love at the age of nine. The Sisters had come with projector and slides and set up their mission in the Village Hall. Somewhere, in an old handbag of treasures and mementoes, there was an autograph book containing the twenty-third psalm calligraphed in Sister Pierce's tiny italic hand.

If only, Pearl was thinking as she refreshed her glass, life was more like the *Bells of St Mary's*, where Bing Crosby tucked Barry Fitzgerald up in bed, crooning an Irish lullaby. Toora-loora-loora.

Luke was flicking through the Yellow Pages. From time to time, unknown to him, a droning like that of a sick mosquito buzzed through his closed lips. There were no witch-doctors listed. He tried the other two local directories with no more success.

'You know what Elvis was saying about . . .'

'Sshh.'

A choirboy was taking a solo. Luke looked away from the screen. He went over to the window, flexing his muscles. He lifted the curtain and let it fall. All that was happening in the street was that the yellow berries on a rowan tree were threatening to ripen in a foreboding of autumn.

'How can you find out something if you don't know where to look?'

'You could try ringing the library information officer. He's supposed to be able to answer queries. What do you want to know?'

'Oh, nothing, really.'

'That's all right then. I rang recently to ask the Meaning of Life. He said he'd call me back but never did.'

'I've got to go to the library anyway tomorrow. Where is it?'

'I'd go to Reigate if I was you, it's bigger and the information service is there.'

'We're going out, Mum.'

Sean and another boy, whom Luke thought to be either the one called Chas or the one called Gaz appeared in the room. How could Pearl remark the unnatural glitter of their eyes when her own were still glazed with unshed tears at the closing hymn?

'Your mascara's streaked, Gaz,' she said.

'So's yours. Goodnight, Mrs Slattery. Thank you for having me,' he added incongruously.

'A pleasure.'

It took but a word of politeness from one of these youths to reinforce her belief that they were all nice lads at heart.

'Your nappy's come unpinned,' she called after him tenderly.

He turned and squinted at the square of tartan pinned to the seat of his jeans.

'Come here, I'll do it for you. I suppose you're off to a Bay City Rollers concert?'

'What?' he asked, as she gave a farewell pat to the jeans in whose pocket reposed a pound note abstracted from her purse. At this casual maternal intimacy Luke rushed from the room but his tormented exit was unnoticed as she sat feeling hopelessly old and outnumbered, remembering how at lunchtime the names of Buddy Holly, the Big Bopper and Richie Valens had been, to everybody present but her, fragments of an unimaginable pre-history, and remembered how she had walked miles over the fields to a friend's house to listen to 'Saturday Club' on her radio. A vivid image of a Fresian cow planted its hooves in front of her. They were cleft and striped like clove humbugs, a bovine visual pun.

Locked in the bathroom where he had bolted Luke stared at his reflection in the door of the bathroom cabinet, a little dovecot of bleached wood which once had been painted white; its speckled glass threw freckles on to his face. Was there anything to distinguish him from the gang of boys who haunted the house? His pale gold hair was not shaved or blue or green or scarlet and did not stand up in black iron spikes like a medieval weapon; a sign of maturity or dullness? Was he what was known in the slang of her day as an old square? His neck rose gracefully, he thought, from the open collar of his shirt; but perhaps she preferred someone hunkier. He couldn't

43

accept that she was immune to his charms, which had seldom failed him before.

Much later he opened the sitting-room door. Pearl and Malcolm from the pub were sitting on the floor eating an Indian take-away with silver foil dishes scattered around them.

'The plimsoll bhaji's not bad,' he seemed to be saying, holding out what looked like a shoe lace on the end of a fork.

'I thought you might like to know,' Luke choked out in a voice clogged with malice, 'that I just found two cigarette packets in Tiffany's room. Empty.'

'Both of them?' asked Pearl. 'Are you sure? What were you doing in Tiffany's room anyway?'

'Looking for something to read.' He became aware of the crumpled copy of *The Naughtiest Girl is a Prefect* in his hand and backed out. In the kitchen he found Tiffany scraping round a foil dish with a spoon while the Siamese cat Cio-Cio-San, wearing a red harness, licked a splodge of curry sauce from her collage. She lifted her head and hissed at Goblin who had walked through the open back door.

'Leave our cat alone!' said Luke.

'Our cat,' corrected Tiffany with a complacent slurp of the spoon.

SIX

*R*IBBONS senior would have been aware that for some time he had been drinking more than he used to if he had let himself, but the days had become blurred and instantly forgotten, like the thriller he was squinting at in the evening light filtering through the yew tree branches outside his window. Bird droppings and streaks of dried rain and smears of last year's berries blotched the panes, and a dead needle, caught by its tip in a cobweb, turned and turned at the glass.

'"Turning and turning in the tightening gyre, the falcon cannot bear the falconer,"' he murmured, congratulating himself on the aptness of the quotation and congratulating himself on the fact that his memory was as sharp as ever, forgetting that he had bungled horribly the marriage service on Saturday and that Rick Ruggles had emerged fully robed from the choir stalls where he had been hiding and tactfully, with a pincer grip on his elbow, suggested that he sit down for a moment in the vestry. He had come to, to find the church deserted and himself going through the pockets of the choir-boys' cassocks. He had lurched from the cracked path, where he had crouched for some time, moved to tears by the poignancy of the confetti, tiny pink and blue and white paper hearts and horseshoes and petals in the dust, poking them with a twig, scooping them into gritty heaps with his hands. Then he stomped into the church hall where the reception was in full swing and homed in on a paper cup of sherry.

'Toast, Father.'

Someone was nudging him.

'Just coffee for me, thanks. Rather a headache . . .' he mumbled, then blinked and realised that he was not at breakfast but surrounded by a *mélange* of plastic spoons and paper plates slimed with trifle and people standing up, shouting, 'The bride and groom!'

'Horse and groom,' he echoed a fraction too late, and looked down to see a cigarette obscenely unrolling in the yellow liquid in his cup.

'Extraordinary,' he said, and stumped out again.

It was a paperback from the library that the Vicar was reading now, bent double, held against the window; too lazy to put on the light. He scratched with his nail at what might have been a droplet of his own or some previous reader's fried breakfast and took a gulp from the mug on his muddled desk. The mug had a sharp projection where its handle had been and a facsimile of an old advertisement for Brasso on its side and, the Vicar reflected, the cheap sherry it contained was probably not dissimilar to the product it advertised. The mug was for the sake of decorum, lest some parishioner should call, but it was rare nowadays that one did. Through the window came the harsh cries of Taskforce at play in the garden.

A son of the manse himself, he had enjoyed a brief flirtation with Rome, abandoned when he had contracted acute rhinitis as the result of an allergy to incense.

'Young Ruggles is a Godsend,' he had often remarked humorously in the early days of Rick's curacy. Now he had lived to eat his words. It had taken Rick Ruggles just two years to change not only the character of the services, but the congregation as well. As the older people first complained that they no longer felt at home in the church where they had worshipped for years and then stayed away altogether as they found themselves ousted from their positions as church-wardens, their names omitted from the flower rotas, instead of being pleased at the sight of his once three-quarters empty church filled with enthusiastic teenagers and young couples with their small noisy children, the Vicar was unhappy. He was embarrassed by their evangelism and suspected that God, whom he had always felt shared most of his ideas, must be too. Ruggles scorned the pulpit; he pranced about the aisles en-couraging his congregation to laugh and clap their hands and join in actions to childish choruses while the Vicar stood sourly to one side, a black gargoyle in his cassock. He had once emerged from the vestry, sermon in hand, to find his church metamorphosed into a barnyard as the congregation clucked and mooed and quacked and bleated, and finally dissolved in a wave of ecumenical laughter as Rick invited them to imper-sonate the hippos entering Noah's ark. He spoke to God less and less, and now they had ceased to communicate at all. The choir had resigned *en masse* and was replaced by a small folk group with harmonicas, recorders and guitars. There was a lot of kissing after Communion, and what the Vicar found har-dest to bear was the fact that they all looked so damned happy.

'The study door opened.

'Oh, it's you.'

'Father, I'd like a word.'

'I wish you wouldn't call me that.'

'Well, you object when I address you as Vicar . . .'

'Naturally. I have a name, like everybody else.'

'Mmm,' said Rick doubtfully as he brushed the seat of the worn chenille sofa before sitting down and leaning forward purposefully, his clasped hands between his widespread knees.

'It's not Advent, is it?' asked the Vicar, before he could speak.

'Of course not. Why?'

'Then why are you wearing that purple tracksuit?'

'Oh, this,' Rick blushed, plucking at his velour knee. 'It was a present.'

'Very nice too,' said the Vicar with sarcastic heartiness, remembering the paltry number of envelopes that had landed in his begging bowl as he sat in the church porch on the last Gift Day. The worst haul ever.

'I want to speak to you about a very serious matter.'

'Speak away, dear boy.'

The Vicar took a gulp of his secret sherry as an anaesthetic against what promised to be a very boring and unpleasant interview.

'It concerns a member of Taskforce . . . A young girl who came to you in distress, seeking help because she'd lost her Faith . . . you told her to look in Lost Property . . .'

'Mmm, yes. I remember – did she find it?'

He picked up the newspaper and studied the back page.

'I just can't get through to you!' Rick leaped to his feet, hitting his palm with his fist. 'Look,' he said, controlling himself, 'suppose we pray together? Now.'

'Have you ever noticed' – the Vicar looked up from his newspaper and took another gulp of sherry – 'the obsession that crossword compilers have with corporal punishment?'

He unscrewed his fountain pen and inserted the word 'thrashing'.

Rick retreated, scarlet-faced, to the door.

'I think it's only fair to tell you that I'm seriously contemplating writing to the Bishop.'

'Give him my regards, and Rick, if you should encounter our esteemed Deaconess on your way out, I wouldn't mind a little something savoury on a tray – Gentleman's Relish on triangles of toast, perhaps, or . . .'

The door slammed behind the curate.

'All that snogging after Eucharist!' shouted the Vicar. 'Do you really think God cares for that sort of thing?'

'Another meaningful dialogue with Rick,' he mused aloud as he stood at the window.

Taskforce was crossing the churchyard, heading for the mini-bus, carrying canoes and paddles over their shoulders, like pickaxes.

'Hi ho, hi ho, it's off to work we go . . .' they sang. They were pretending to be the Seven Dwarfs. Rick brought up the rear, an orange lifejacket over his purple tracksuit, a canoe on his head.

'Which one is that dwarf that everybody always forgets, whose name no one can remember?' the Vicar wondered. 'Let's see – sloth, gluttony, lust . . . oh hell . . .'

Two slender nymphs in shorts raced past, waving their paddles with a cry of 'Swallows and Amazons forever!' The Vicar sighed and turned away; he lit his pipe to fumigate the intolerably long summer evening but could not silence with his smoke the blackbird singing in the pear tree.

' "There's the wise thrush . . ." '

He clenched his teeth on his pipe stem, yellow and decayed against the last white drift of blossom falling, falling past the window.

Cherry stood uncertainly by the rear of the mini-bus, looking fragile in the bulky lifejacket and sawn-off jeans.

'You don't look too happy. Anything I can do?'

Rick put a comradely arm round her shoulder.

'I'm a bit nervous. It's just that I . . . I can't swim.' The blush ran up her face and down her neck as she kicked at the gravel with her plimsoll.

'You'd better come in the two-seater with me,' said Rick.

SEVEN

EVERY morning the bathroom carpet, now unrecognisable as the enormous festive Swiss roll once carried in triumph shoulder-high from Allders, was laced with silvery trails. When Luke inquired, at breakfast on Monday, about these nocturnal traces he was told by Tiffany that they were left by a visitor named Sally Slug. She was corrected by Sean, frowsting over his fried bread in the jumble sale long johns he wore as pyjamas.

'It's Trail the Snail.'

'Oh shut up, the pair of you.' Pearl slammed the frying pan into the sink in anger at the reference to this molluscular invasion, which might symbolise all the inadequacies of their lifestyle. The front of her dressing-gown was engulfed in a tidal wave of greasy water. She had found a blade of grass growing beside the bath, under which, presumably, their moist house guest had retreated from the morning sun. She was working a day shift that week, from ten o'clock to two.

'This iron's hopeless!' Cherry banged it down on the iron-ing board, abandoning the attempt to expunge the creases of the launderette from a school blouse. 'Can't we get a new one?'

'Oh yes, certainly. I'll put it on my shopping list along with the video and dishwasher and microwave oven.' The sun which shone blearily through the kitchen window dappled by splashes from the sink sketched the beginning of a jagged headache over one eye and for some reason recalled to her a shameful day not long ago when undone by Belle Cave and loneliness, she had dialled the Samaritans. The man who took the call had been very understanding, his name was John, and he had spoken quietly and soothingly to her, assuring her that she was a worthwhile person, and was on the verge of persuading her through her tears that life was worth living when he had broken off, then . . .

'What's that noise at your end, Helen?'

She had had the foresight to provide herself with an alias, actually the Weasel's name.

'What noise?'

'A sort of crunching . . .'

'I'm just eating a bit of fried bread.'

She had heard the line go dead. She had tried to ring him back to explain that there was a respectable historical precedent – the condemned man ate a hearty breakfast – but the line had been engaged.

As Luke approached the library he could hear a steady thud thud thud followed by a crash. A huge iron ball suspended in chains from a crane was attacking the back of the Majestic Cinema and people stood in the street to watch, with bits of art deco falling round their heads. The auditorium was exposed, tiers of seats sagged naked to the sky while the ball bashed and bounced off a sagging iron girder. Side-stepping a falling brick, he went up the steps into the library.

'I'd like to join the library,' he said to a small woman nervously shuffling tickets behind the counter.

'Are you sure?' she asked, convulsively masticating several little yellow balls of Double Amplex.

As he gave his surprised assent he saw that she had attempted to cheer up her surgical neck collar with a wisp of fuchsia chiffon.

'If you'd like to go over to the desk,' she whispered, 'the library manager will deal with you.'

Luke joined a small queue of what looked almost like penitents and studied the library manager behind the desk. Her silver hair was caught up in a shining chignon secured with small weapons and she wore a quasi-military blue dress studded with silver buttons on chest and epaulets. Luke was wondering idly if epaulets had been designed solely to be struck off at the point of a sword at a later date, when he became aware of the conversation in front of him.

'I'm afraid that's just not good enough,' the library manager was saying. 'Two Doris Lessings and one Simone de Beauvoir. Next!'

'Mrs Kennedy used to let us choose our own books,' quavered the woman thus addressed.

'I'm afraid things got altogether too slack under Mrs Kennedy's regime. Next! Must I explain again, Mr Baker?' She smiled wearily at the ancient who shuffled up, placing his trembling hands on her desk for support. 'The county has instituted this system of double fines for the over-seventies on the grounds that they are old enough to know better. Now, do you want your tickets back or not?'

'I'd like to join the library, please,' said Luke less confidently than at first, when his turn came.

'Are you over sixteen? Are you a permanent resident of the borough and have you proof of address?'

Luke drew himself up and clicked his heels.

'*Jawöhl, mein Führer!*'

Five minutes later Luke found himself in possession of six green book tickets and three yellow audio tickets. As he turned to go upstairs to Non-fiction with Cherry's list in his hand he collided with a wild-eyed woman who all but prostrated herself at the desk.

'I'm so sorry I'm late,' she babbled, 'I've got a migraine and . . .'

'There's no such thing as a migraine, Susan. It's all in your head.' She tapped her own silvery coiffs. 'In your head. I've put you down to tidy Sport, Craft, Rel. and Bel. until twelve o'clock. Then you'd better pack the van in lieu of lunch.' The little lady in the surgical collar gave her colleague a silent sympathetic look as she staggered past her with two armfuls of enormous volumes. She recalled the day when Mrs Kennedy and most of the then existing staff had been driven away in a yellow van, with the entwined oak leaves of Surrey County Council emblazoned on the side, never to return.

When Luke came to have his books stamped out he heard the old lady in front of him whisper 'I'm not really very keen on patio gardening and yoga, dear.'

'Never mind,' the assistant whispered back, slipping two Mills and Boons furtively into her basket.

Then Luke, in pursuit of the chief aim of his trip to the library sought the information officer. There was nobody at the Information Centre. He wandered round the Music section and chose three cassettes, pondering the wisdom of an alliance with a woman whose All-Time Top Ten contained 'Old Shep', 'Honey' and 'Seasons in the Sun', the one-time secretary of the Redhill chapter of the Andy Fairweather-Low Fan Club. He noticed, as he rotated the cassette stand, a blind man riffling through the Talking Books. In his hand were three yellow audio tickets marked with a red cross. His own were not so marked. He concluded that the red cross must be of some significance so he borrowed a red pen from the frightened woman at the desk and in the privacy of the Children's section, criss-crossed his own tickets. There was still nobody at the Information Centre and the telephone was off the hook. He took his cassette cases to the counter.

'That will be sixty pence, please,' she said as she stamped them. He handed her his tickets. She looked at them. 'Oh, I'm sorry. I didn't realise. No charge.' He felt it best to leave at once, wondering as he went, how long it would be before blind people were charged double for their cassettes and records on the grounds that they had developed a more acute sense of hearing than sighted persons.

*

When Luke emerged into the town he noticed a marked change in the population. Young people filled the streets. A crowd of students from the Sixth-form College and Grammar School sprawled on the steps of the Old Town Hall, the benches and pavement, taking their lunchtime ease in shorts, drinking from cans, eating ice-cream, laughing. For the first time he regretted discontinuing his formal education as he walked past them unnoticed, alienated and feeling old, hurrying back to Pearl.

As he passed Shaw's Corner, all at once a crack of thunder split the sky, lightning bounced off the pavement in front of him and great flaccid drops of rain soaked him and drenched the naked bronze man, thrusting a little child to the traffic, on the war memorial. As he squelched along he indulged in a fantasy homecoming in which Pearl threw open the front door.

'You're soaked to the skin. Let's get those wet clothes off you . . .'

In fact he had to stand on the doorstep ringing the bell for five minutes before she answered the door. Meanwhile the sun came out and set everything steaming. He followed her into the kitchen.

'I've had a bloody day,' she said while he tried to strike an insouciant attitude as he dripped.

'A nail-file was found in a bar of butterscotch and we've been reported to the Inspector of Health. Heads will roll. I've just washed this bloody floor, do you have to walk all over it?'

Luke felt he ought to be able to say something like 'You're magnificent when you're angry,' but, tongue-tied, he took off his shoes and paddled miserably to his room.

Pearl's temper was not improved when the Weasel arrived uninvited to bear her off to the Parents' Evening at Tiffany's school. Although, like the library lady, she had taken the precaution of a handful of Double Amplex, she feared that last night's curry was on her breath and in consequence hardly dared open her mouth and listened dumbly to a list of her daughter's shortcomings, going off into a sort of daydream as she stared at a display of coats of arms which the children had concocted for themselves. She decided not to risk seeking Tiffany's.

'. . . problems at home,' the teacher, a young girl with a sincere pony tail was saying.

'What?' How could she know about Sally Slug and Trail the Snail?

She sat silently beside the Weasel in the Range Rover on the drive home, head averted to prevent wafts of garlic steaming up the windscreen and consolidating the Weasel's opinion of her.

'Isobel's decided to go in for Oxbridge,' the Weasel was saying.

'What? Oh. Is that good or bad?'

'Well, it depends on how you look at it,' she replied somewhat huffily. 'Of course it means a lot of jolly hard work, but she's got the ability if she – this is your house, isn't it?'

The Range Rover brought its absurdly high wheels to a halt.

'Yes, lovely, thank you. I don't suppose you want to come in. I expect you've got lots to do.'

'Well, just a very quick coffee would be lovely . . . I hate these affairs, don't you? A total waste of time. I mean, if your child's got problems you'll be in touch with the school anyway and the parents they really need to see are the ones who won't bother to come.'

This diatribe saw them out of the car and in Pearl's case, desperately, into the kitchen.

'I don't suppose you'd like a glass of wine?' she said. 'We seem to be out of coffee. Of course I could send someone out for some . . .'

'Oh don't go to any trouble. A glass of wine would be super,' said the Weasel with an air of bravado, imagining perhaps a tulip of chilled Liebfraumilch served on a white table floating in the scented dusk of a flower-encompassed patio.

Enter Tiffany on roller boots propelled through the door by Cherry.

'Mum, if Miss Marshall said I did anything, I didn't, and if she said I didn't do anything, I did.'

'Mum, is there any of that nit shampoo left? My head feels as if it's really crawling . . .' Cherry began. 'Oh, hello, Mrs Headley-Jones. Mum, Precious is here, she brought some beans from the garden.'

'I don't think you've met my daughter-in-law Precious, have you, Mrs Headley-Jones?' said Pearl struggling desperately with the corkscrew as Precious walked in.

'Pleased to meet you. I've been going to a most interesting evening class on "The Making of the Surrey Landscape",' Mrs Headley-Jones found herself saying to no one in particular as she took a gulp from her thick glass of red plonk.

'And this must be your son?' she said brightly as Luke walked in.

'Oh no, he's the lodger. And his name's Luke, not Roger,' answered Pearl in an ill-judged attempt at levity inspired by a too-deep draught of Belle Cave on an empty stomach. Luke shot her a grimace which was caught by the Weasel and sat down at the table beside Precious. She yawned.

'God, I'm tired. Our Ward Sister's off sick and I've been run off my feet. Mum, when you gonna get some decent glasses? I'd be ashamed to use these old things – what your friend must think . . .'

'What do you mean, off sick?'

Luke grabbed the bottle and poured some more into Precious's glass.

'Who can say? Very mysterious, ha ha ha.' She shook with laughter and the blue beads in her hair clashed. Their heads bent together over the table.

'Why don't we take our glasses into the other room, Mrs Headley-Jones?' said Pearl rising and taking the bottle.

'Mmm, super. I hope you don't mind my saying so, but do you think you should let Tiffany kiss the cat like that? Have you any idea how many diseases are passed from cats to humans?'

'More people kill cats than cats kill people,' replied Pearl darkly as she led the way.

'I do so agree,' said the Weasel with an earnestness that to Pearl seemed slightly early in the evening for she had drunk but one glass of wine. 'I say, just a drop, thanks. Mustn't forget I'm driving. I feel slightly squiffy, oh dear. I left a casserole for my mob to fend for themselves. I do so agree, it's all wrong to give pets as presents, I mean people are so irresponsible and it's not they who have to pick up the bill when the animal has to be put down, is it?'

In the kitchen Luke was scribbling down a name and address from Precious's dictation.

The next morning Helen Headley-Jones, in her *Guardian* jogging suit, sat at her kitchen table in a warm soapy smell of scrubbed wood watching a faint steam that rose from the damp grooves that marked the newspaper spread out in front of her and dissolved in the morning sunshine. Helen Headley-Jones was the daughter of a now-retired shopkeeper whose wartime activities had earned him the title of Butcher of Merstham. The scrubbed pine table at which she was seated had come from his shop and had been, perforce, stained a deep red. The secret of her perfect pastry was the marble slab on which her cool fingers moulded it. Sometimes, although she had become a Social Democrat, she gloomily compared her own career with that of a certain grocer's daughter from Grantham.

The market for crinolined toilet-roll covers seemed to have dried up so she was pleased to have coerced Pearl Slattery into crocheting those toy clowns for the fête but had to suppress a nagging fear that they would be gaudy raggedy creatures who would somehow behave disgracefully and disrupt her stall.

She read, with faint puzzlement, a review of a life of Alma Mahler: something seemed not quite right. As she folded the newspaper she realised that she had not, as she had thought, been reading about Cosima Wagner and the lines between her brows smoothed out as she began to hum and stack the dishwasher. She thought about the previous evening: that odd sulky boy who was the lodger and that black person whose name she thought had been Precious and who, incredibly, had addressed Pearl Slattery as Mum. She compared the rackety Slattery household with her own ordered habitat and she felt oddly depressed. Perhaps it was that dire red plonk she had consumed so enthusiastically; the dregs clogging her brain were giving her a dull headache as she moved about the house trying to dispel the post-plonk anxiety with cleaning materials. Helen tried hard to be good. Several times a week with guilt sitting beside her in the passenger seat she zig-zagged across the borough with foil dishes of food slopping in the boot delivering Meals on Wheels, and sometimes in recompense might be shown an ulcerated leg or thermal bandage. She tore carefully the stamps from her letters to give to the Diabetics; saved her old newspapers for the Scouts; took her glass bottles to the bottle bank in Sainsbury's car park once a week; and yet sometimes, as on this morning, she felt that she had no right to breathe too much of the earth's oxygen, as if she used up too many of the world's resources without contributing enough. She even envied Pearl Slattery her job at Snashfold's. She felt that it gave her a status and identity that she herself did not possess. 'I've got to go to Marks and Sparks' did not have the same ring as 'I've got to go to work.'

On her way to the compost heap Helen stopped to bury her face in a rose bush. Pleasure mingled with pain; not only the thorn in the tip of her nose, but the fact that years ago she had, uncharacteristically, nipped a cutting from the Chelsea Flower Show. Now she attempted to atone by pressing swaying bunches of its heavy blooms on to neighbours and friends. Its scent was too sweet, almost decadent in the air that already threatened to become too hot.

'Mum, I've asked you not to iron creases in my jeans!'

It was her daughter, Isobel, supposedly on study leave,

leaning out of her bedroom window, waving the jeans at her and wearing a shirt casually and wrongly buttoned.

'Put some clothes on at once,' hissed Helen.

'Oh for God's sake!'

Isobel slammed the window. Helen looked round fearfully lest anyone had seen this exchange but a thrush attacking a snail was her only witness and it flew away squawking over the long wide lawn to the safety of a flower bed.

'If you must eat snails,' called Helen, picking up the disgusting broken mess and flinging it after the bird, 'you could at least tidy up the shells!' She went in to wash her hands and encountered Isobel slopping boiling water from the kettle on to a tea bag. A dross of sugar frosted the work top.

'I'll thank you never to speak to me in that tone of voice again, madam.'

'God!'

'And blaspheming. What's got into you lately? You've become so rough and rude, almost, yes – I have to say it – graceless.' Her voice trembled. 'I'm going shopping. Clear up this mess and get some decent clothes on. This sloppy attitude isn't going to help with your A-levels, you know.'

She didn't trust herself to speak further and was at the garage door before she burst into tears and realised she had forgotten the car keys.

'We're turning into the Slatterys,' she said aloud, before scrubbing at her eyes with a tissue and beaming her brightest smile on a passing neighbour who almost recoiled from the glare. She would have been surprised to learn that Cherry Slattery had renounced blasphemy at almost the same time as her own daughter had taken it up.

She walked along lost in her thoughts towards Reigate, oblivious that she might strike an observer as an erratic figure, thrusting her long neck into a spray of flowers, catching an overhanging branch and stripping the bitter scented flowering currant leaves through her fingers. She was resolving to make up the silly quarrel with Isobel as soon as the child apologised and anticipating the shamefaced hug with which she would greet her mother, when a pair of collared doves fluttered across her path and settled on a roof, reminding her of another couple who used to visit her garden, whom she had named Valentine and Valentine, after the legend that the birds mate on St Valentine's Day, and would sit on her roof going hoo hoo hoo for hours, sending melancholy spirals of sound down the chimney. The birds turned her thoughts to other pigeons, as she strode, that she had seen a few days ago at Victoria Station hobbling about on feet burned by repellents to nubbed clumps of dirty coral. She had been on a rare visit to London, which she hated, was frightened by, and which always gave her a headache. The indicator board rolled up its slats as one by one the trains were cancelled and the concourse filled with stoic commuters; there was nowhere to sit, for all the benches were occupied by vagrants, none of whom had the courtesy to move themselves or their belongings to accommodate a foot-sore lady hung about with Harrod's carrier bags. How odd, she thought, for those who were going nowhere to choose a place crowded with people who had somewhere to go and whose skis and backpacks, sun hats, toy donkeys, briefcases and newspapers must only point up their plight.

That morning her husband Jeremy had told her that they must entertain a colleague and his wife. She was wondering if she could get away with wearing her new sprigged cotton nightdress to Glyndebourne or if she would create the impression of a grey-haired milkmaid, minus yoke and pails but clutching a bottle of champagne and wicker picnic basket; and if she scrubbed out the basket, which she had used to carry the cat to the vet, the smell of disinfectant would have faded or would taint the strawberries. Suddenly she stopped, snuffling a leaf from her nose, aware of someone following her, afraid that she had been talking to herself or even whistling a snatch of Janáček, and turned round. Some yards behind, a figure in a long stained coat was raking through the litter bin growling a monotone through tattooed lips. Helen stood staring in safety because he was so absorbed in what he was doing, throwing discarded garbage on to the path. Time and dirt had made dreadlocks of his hair. A cider bottle stuck out of his pocket. 'A vagrant. In Reigate,' she murmured; a sign of the times. She supposed that he was just passing through; surely he could not be an inhabitant, but she shuddered as though he carried the plague in the black skirts of his long coat. Was anywhere safe, if not Reigate? Her fingers closed on the purse lying in her shopping basket to make sure it was invisible. 'You ought to be ashamed of yourself,' she told herself sternly. She took out a pound note and put it back. A pound wouldn't do him any good at all. While she agonised, almost dancing on the blue asphalt, the man sank down in the shrubbery with a retrieved copy of the *Sun* and put the bottle to his lips. Helen saw that she was standing by a bench. She laid fifty pence on the seat and impulsively added a packet of Ryvita. As she passed the telephone box on the corner she saw that someone had stuck a sticker on the glass: 'Smile. Jesus loves you.' Helen smiled. She thought that after all she might nip into Crawley to change a cardigan.

She remembered with pleasure that it was her French conversation class that evening: *'Cette après-midi, j'ai rencontré un clochard. En Reigate, de toutes places! Zut alors, sacrebleu!'*

'Izzie,' she called, running into the house, quite forgetting their quarrel, 'what's the past participle of *rencontrer*?' But Isobel wasn't there.

A pall of disgrace hung over the room when Pearl woke that same morning. She untangled herself from the sheets to knock the alarm clock on to its pompous face and reach for the glass of water she had placed beside the bed. As she drank a multicoloured fear floated into her mind causing her to choke. Reason told her that she could not have promised to crochet some toy clowns for the SDP fête, but experience said that probably she had. The Weasel's own speciality was toilet-roll covers in the shape of crinolined ladies in delicate shades of green and mauve and yellow foam rubber. There was a dead one in the corner of the Slatterys' bathroom. What confidences had been weaseled out of her, she wondered as she stared at her outstretched leg, whose toes needed repainting. They had touched on the great truths, she remembered as she drank; that one could get drunk on water if one drank enough, or fat on lettuce, that it was true, as claimed in the ad, that it was more economical to buy one more-expensive washing-up liquid than two cheapies; and they had pondered the great imponderables such as reincarnation and the fact that there was always one teaspoon left in the bottom of the washing-up bowl when you thought you'd finished, that the red flowers of the poinsettia were really coloured bracts . . . but what else? She feared that they had exchanged a kiss at the front door. How they would avoid each other's eyes at their next meeting. What did it matter, she thought as she passed to the bathroom, a minor disaster surely, compared with being accused of being drunk in charge of a Safeway's trolley. That charge had been dropped but the pain lingered on. She pulled at the dead lady in the corner of the bathroom intending to get rid of it and the reminder of its provenance, but its skirt was blackened and stuck with mildew to the skirting board. Avoiding the scales, she stepped dispiritedly into the bath and began to wash the soap.

'I got it in Pendereds' sale,' she heard the Weasel saying as she smoothed her creaseless dress over a brown knee, 'reduced to £17.99, and it's very good-tempered, I just bung it in the machine.' Her eyes turned to the brimming launderette bag of dirty washing. The tip of a moist tail flicked under the bath.

'But I can't crochet,' Pearl wailed aloud and lay back almost drowned by the thought of her children, none of whom she had taught to knit or sew or crochet or cook, although Cherry could make a perfect batch of Viota fairy cakes when she had a mind to. Pearl resolved to set her house in order; to write to Jack, who, she feared, must be coming near to the end of his sentence, to have her hair cut, to clean the oven and order some new stretch covers from the catalogue for the sofa and chairs in the front room. Except that she couldn't pay for them. And there was no oven-cleaner.

★

Jaki's Hair Salon wasn't even much cheaper than the more glamorous establishments in Redhill. Pearl patronised it out of habit and a misplaced sense of loyalty. She sat waiting to be shorn, reading an ancient copy of *Woman's Weekly*, keeping her head down to avoid having to speak to the woman sitting next to her, with tufts of hair sticking through the holes in a plastic cap. The salon was crowded, the clientele was elderly, for it was cheap rate for pensioners' day, and although a curling sign in the window said Unisex, it was entirely female. Pearl was being fitted in, and she felt it, cramped between the woman with the false scalp whose tufts were being tinted as pink as the cover of *Woman's Weekly*, and another with a grey hood clamped over her head, a hairnet peeping from its rim.

Jaki approached, tiny on her stiletto heels, the handle of a steel comb sticking like a dagger from the pocket of her overall, scissors, snipping the air.

'Sure you don't want me to wash it for you? Cut and blow-dry?'

'No, just a dry trim, thanks.'

'Please yourself, only it makes it much easier to cut.'

Pearl shook her head and the scissors grazed her neck. She wanted to keep the price down, and feared the painful pressure of the sink on the back of her neck, grinding the vertebrae and cutting off the blood to the brain.

'It's really raggy and out of condition. Who done it for you last time?'

'You did.'

There was silence from Jaki as she wrenched the hair straight up from Pearl's forehead in the comb and stared at it critically. Pearl averted her eyes from the mirror and stared at a plant expiring under the grey ruched net curtain that obscured half the window and filtered the cruel sunlight.

'Don't object, do you? I'm gasping.'

Jaki lit a cigarette. Pearl did not object; it masked the smell of sweat and might act as a gag against the topic of holidays.

'Been away yet this year?' The cigarette wobbled up and down as she worked.

'Not yet.'

A young girl was serving cups of tea to favoured customers under the driers, balancing cups and saucers and a milk bottle and sugar packet on a small tray. Ash fell on to Pearl's hair.

'Ever thought of having grey low-lights put in?' Jaki asked as she brushed it away.

She held up a hand-mirror to the back of Pearl's butchered head and stepped back with professional pride, into the tea-tray. A white parabola of milk shot across the room as cups crashed; there was a scream, a bang and a flash. Pearl tore off her plastic bib and escaped in the confusion and smell of burning plastic.

'Yoohoo.' It was the voice of the Weasel.

Pearl turned in mid-flight, brushing at her shoulders.

'I'm just going to Marks to take back a cardi. Would you like to come?'

'I haven't got anything to take back.'

'Well, you could buy something today and take it back next time.'

Last night's kiss melted in the hot air that smelled of ice-cream.

'I don't think I've got time. I've got to work later,' she lied.

'I'm only going to Crawley, we'll be back in good time for the kids.'

'I don't think . . .'

'Oh well, I just thought it might make a change for you. Must dash, I'm double-parked.'

She dashed, in pursuit of her hobby, to the Weaselmobile, double-parked head and shoulders above the other cars. Pearl went into a newsagent's and bought a black and white aerial view of old Redhill. In the post office she stared at it, thinking that she had nothing at all to say to Jack. At last she wrote in her big writing: 'Having a wonderful time. Wish you were here.' There was still a lot of space, so she added: 'Redhill has changed a lot since this photograph was taken,' signed her name, addressed it to HM Prison, and satisfied that duty had been done, stuck on a second-class stamp and dropped it into the box.

Back at home her satisfaction with her afternoon's work was short-lived. As she ran distracted fingers through her hair in front of the kitchen mirror, she reeled back in anguish from a scattering of dark hairs, victims of Jaki the grim reaper, adhering to her upper lip, which the Weasel must have seen, and taken for natural growth. There was no doubt about it, she looked quite hideous. Her hair had looked perfectly all right before. She went over to the sink and attacked a pile of slightly wizened potatoes with the pan scourer.

EIGHT

I*T WAS* late afternoon by the time Luke reached Reigate, after calling in at the Job Centre and signing on. Reigate was quite different from Redhill, he observed again. He heard a young mother refuse to buy her child a packet of Outer Spacers, on the grounds that they contained too much food colouring and offered an unsulphured apricot as a substitute. Reigate made him uneasy. He bought himself a Slush Puppy; shades of Tiffany, he thought, swallowing the blue ice, as he paused to study the inscription under the statue of Dame Margot Fonteyn; tricklets of sweat ran into her vaporous bronze dress as she pirouetted in the sun. There was a glass jug threaded with pink swirls that he would have liked to buy for Pearl in the window of an antique shop, but it was closed and the price tag read six pounds. Holmesdale Road was a long fascinating jumble of architectural styles, with a cat sprawled on almost every windowsill or path; there was a newsagent's, a post office, a greengrocer's, a handsome red-brick tiled butcher's shop opposite the little station where a diesel train throbbed alongside the platform, a school, a cobbler's, a strange shop selling bows and arrows with a faded picture of a fox with a target drawn on its body; tiny terraced houses hung with creepers and flowering briers, passion flowers and quinces, cottages and square elegant Georgian houses with their names lettered in the glass above the pediment. Luke remembered that he had once wanted to study architecture, wondered if it was too late, and dismissed the thought as too difficult. He pitched his empty Slush carton into a bin outside the little brother of the bigger newsagent, and exchanged a word with a tortoiseshell cat. The address he was seeking turned out, disappointingly, to be in a small block of purpose-built flats, pink and yellow like a Battenberg cake. Number four was distinguished from its neighbours only by a little black doorknocker in the shape of a human skull. Luke put out his hand to lift it, hesitated, and chose instead the bell at the side of the door. Two-tone chimes sounded through the flat. The door was opened by an orange man, not the Ulster variety, although Luke could not of course guess at his politics yet, but the Old Reigatean tie knotted tightly round the neck of his white shirt would have given a clue to a more sophisticated observer. Some quirk of pigmentation had dyed his hair orange and scattered rusty pinpoints across the coarse peel of his face. The overall impression was of a genial little gingerbread man fresh from the oven and a spicy smell drifted out of the kitchen.

'Major Moth?'

'Yes?'

'I'm sorry to intrude on you but . . .'

'I don't see anyone without an appointment.' He started to close the door.

'Please. It's really urgent.'

'It always is. Good day.'

'Precious gave me your name,' Luke said desperately as the door painfully pinched his foot.

'How do you know Precious? Are you a friend?'

'I'm her future father-in-law!'

'You mean, brother-in-law?'

The door eased slightly its pressure.

'No.'

'You'd better come in.'

Luke followed him into the kitchen fearful of finding a black trussed cockerel that he would have to rescue, rushing to the window and throwing it fluttering and squawking into the air; or a smoking chalice, a candelabrum with seven black candles. The spicy scent came not from exotic cones of incense but from a fruitcake, cooling on a rack on the gleaming work top.

'Sit down.'

Luke sat on a brown and orange check vinyl and chrome stool at the table. Through the window he saw a blue rotary clothesline fold down like a parasol and a pair of hands in pink rubber gloves slide a protective plastic sheath over its spokes.

'Well?'

Luke fixed his eyes on the Beverley Nichols' Cat Calendar on the wall.

'Well, I'm in love with this woman . . .'

'And she does not return your affection?'

'Right. She doesn't even . . . I mean, she just . . .'

'What makes you think I can help?'

'You helped Precious. She told me. You put a curse or something on that nurse for her – and you caused . . .'

'A small triumph, certainly. But why should I help you, white youth with blue lips, who either suffers from a heart condition or has been eating a raspberry Slush Puppy, who has in his pocket tainted money stolen from the very person he seeks to charm?'

'It's only fifty pence,' Luke mumbled devastated. 'I was going to give it back, I've just signed on. I won't get any money until next week.' He licked his lips and wiped them with the back of his hand.

The toaster, saucepans and kettle were of a mushroom shade, garnished with unevocative brown ears of corn.

'Did you really imagine that you could buy my services for fifty pence?'

'It was all there was.' Luke hung his head and traced circles on the table with his finger. He wanted to run away but didn't dare; he felt that he could not stand up if he tried. Judged by a

68

gingerbread man and found wanting; talks in his father's study, feet-shuffling interviews in front of headmasters' desks, the police station, the courtroom, the governors' room at Stillwood Hall, and always he had behaved shamefully, shabbily. He felt like a character in a book of Tiffany's, one of Whyteleafe School's few failures, dispatched with his trunk in a taxi in the disgraceful grey dawn, before the grave announcement in morning assembly.

'Give me your hand,' said Major Moth suddenly.

As his hand lay like a dead crab on the pink palm and an orange finger traced his lines of love and fate, Luke saw Pearl as he had seen her that morning as clearly as if she had been standing in that ordinary kitchen, in front of him. A dried tomato seed was caught in the gold braid of her dressing-gown, her bare feet left a faint frosting of talc on the kitchen floor as she padded from table to grill. Pins and needles were pricking the elbow that rested on the table. He looked into the Major's face and saw not a glimmer of humour or good humour in the twinkling amber eyes. His hand was dropped; he rubbed his tingling palm.

'Give it to me straight, Doc, I can take it. How long have I got?' he said with a nervous laugh.

'If I knew, I wouldn't tell you. It's a question of professional ethics. I've decided to trust you. I shall give you what you ask, but be warned, it's very potent stuff, not to be used lightly. Understand?'

He stared into Luke's eyes for what seemed like several minutes. Then, as if satisfied, he went over to the fridge and took out a jug. He filled a little glass bottle with blue liquid and stopped it with a cork.

'This stuff costs five pounds a fluid ounce,' he said. 'There is enough for two doses here. I'll send you a bill for the potion and for my consultation fee, which you will, of course, settle promptly.' He handed the bottle to Luke, who read the label: 'The Elixir'. He longed to ask what the Major had seen in his hand and why he had changed his mind, but didn't like to.

'Thank you very much.'

He stood awkwardly, fingering a bean which lay on the table. It broke into halves and a tiny white elephant fell out.

'Oh, I'm sorry.'

'It doesn't matter.' The Major fitted the bean together. 'Take it. It will bring you luck. It's a very rare charm from the East.'

As Luke walked home he stifled a memory of a turbaned pedlar at the Vicarage door sifting a handful of such beans through his fingers. He hurried past four women in straw hats, holding Bibles, emerging from a strict Baptist Chapel. The sky was performing an extravaganza of turquoise and mother of pearl as Luke neared home; clouds heaped like shells over Redhill. He raided an abandoned garden and stole an armful of white flowers. Pearl took a step back when she opened the front door to him. Lilac and May. What could be unluckier?

The heavy flowers loaded with doom and sweet and bitter scent, already past their best, crossed the threshold and were thrust into her arms.

'No. No. Get them out!'

He staggered backwards as they were shoved into his face and sat down heavily, scratched and bleeding among the broken blossoms as Pearl turned at a cry from the interior and disappeared into the house. He kicked the flowers.

'You'll be sorry!' he muttered as he took out the little bottle and held it up to the light. Her attack bewildered him. He had no idea that it was the flowers and not himself that had provoked it, not knowing that it was thought unlucky to bring lilac and hawthorn into the house. It must be that she had discovered the fifty pence piece was missing. Again he was unaware that Pearl scarcely ever knew how much money she ought to have, lurching from one monetary crisis to another in a blizzard of bills, living on credit from one Giro or payslip to the next.

The smell of hardboiled eggs hit him as he slunk into the kitchen with petals stuck to the sole of his shoe. It was salad for tea. Pearl was washing a lettuce under the tap, Tiffany chopping the leaves off radishes with a blunt knife.

'Mrs Headley-Jones makes roses out of radishes,' she remarked as she popped one into her own red mouth.

'But can she make radishes out of roses?' replied her mother.

'I don't know.'

'There you are then!'

She shook the lettuce sending a triumphant shower round the kitchen.

Tiffany could not answer for her teeth were now embedded in a bar of Snashfold's Premium Jawbreaker, Toffee of Champions. Generations of Redhill children had cut their teeth, and their tongues, on Snashfold's sweets, but now the once-mighty company supplier of sweets to *le tout* Surrey was in decline. Carriages had once swept up to the great wrought-iron factory gates; now there were no gates, Snashfold's was enclosed by buildings and what was left of its garden, designed by the original Josiah Snashfold, a converted Quaker, for the pleasure of his workers, was a car park where a single mutilated lime tree dropped sticky splotches from its sickly stumps on to the cars below it and a broken fountain clogged with leaves and litter. There had been some redundancies and there was talk of forming a workers' co-operative if the factory was forced to close. Pearl thought this was foolish; there was already the Co-op in London Road and that didn't seem to be doing very well; witness the sad headline in the *Surrey Mirror:* CO-OP RAIDED: NOTHING TAKEN.

'Mother!' Cherry came into the kitchen and prodded the potatoes whose skins were slipping off and insides disintegrating into a floury fibrous mass. 'I think these potatoes are done. Mother, do you think it's altogether healthy for Sean and Chas to go on showering together at their age?'

Pearl had noticed that Cherry had taken to addressing her as 'Mother' since she had become a member of St Elmo's Church.

'Oh, well, in this hot weather . . .' she mumbled.

Her handbag stood open-mouthed on the table. He had to

try to insert what was left of her money. Cherry caught him eyeing the bag. He blushed.

'What exactly did you say you were inside for?' she asked.

'Nothing much. I'll tell you sometime.' He turned to Pearl. 'You've had your hair cut?'

'I liked it better before,' said Tiffany. 'It makes you look older.'

'Thanks a lot!'

Luke wanted to put his arm around her, to pull the sadistically shorn head to rest on his chest, to comfort her. She had no one to look after her. His mouth was dry; his hands hung stiffly at his sides like the stuffed gloves of a guy. He put one of them into his pocket to find his lucky charm. Fluff, crumbs, chewing gum, a half-pence piece, shreds of tobacco.

'What's up with you?' asked Pearl sharply.

'Nothing, I just can't find something. It must be here somewhere.'

'I expect it'll turn up,' she said flatly.

'What was it?'

'A lucky charm.'

'We all lose our charms in the end.'

'Are you crying about your hair?' asked Tiffany.

'It's the spring onions,' said Pearl, but she turned from the mirror and rushed out of the room. At least the little bottle was still there. He held it up to the light throwing splashes of cobalt blue around the room.

'What's that?' Tiffany grabbed at the bottle.

He held it above his head. 'Get off!'

Her sharp little fingers pinched his arm. 'It's food colouring. Give us a taste!'

'No, you can't. It's medicine.'

'Go on, just a lick. I love medicine!'

He managed to get it back into his pocket and thrust Tiffany on to a chair. The consequences of her swallowing the love potion were too horrible to contemplate.

★

Ten minutes later Cherry came into the front room to find her mother lying red-eyed on the sofa, dappled by the light filtered by the leaves of the rose bushes outside the window. In the street a beer can clinked, kicked about by a gang of boys with a vicious metallic sound in a fusillade of raw laughter.

'Hello darling, had a good day?' Pearl swallowed on the anxiety that like an unpleasant wad of chewing gum was always in her mouth these days in Cherry's company since she had joined St Elmo's congregation.

'Overcome by onions,' she explained.

'What? Mother . . . ?'

Pearl swung her legs to the floor and stood up.

'What, my love?'

'Do you think I could have some money?'

'Of course. How much?' She saw her purse gaping like a dead fish on the kitchen table.

'Twenty pounds.'

'What on earth for?'

'Taskforce is having a Christian houseparty in Essex.'

'Seems a long way to go.'

'Oh it doesn't matter. Forget it. I knew I wouldn't be able to go.'

Cherry slammed out of the room. Pearl ran after her and pulled her back by the wrist.

'What do you mean, you knew you wouldn't be able to go?'

'Well, it's obvious isn't it?'

Like a drowning person, Pearl saw a dirty river of empty bottles and cigarette packets gush past her eyes. Clenching one fist to her side, she placed the other on her daughter's rigid shoulder.

'Of course you can go. I'll get the money, OK?'

'Thanks, Mum.'

Pearl saw the flushed flawless skin of her cheek, the drowned blue of her eyes, then she felt Cherry's shoulder relax as a current of their old easy love flowed through her. She went back to the kitchen humming a cheerful, desperate tune, as she put out of her mind the total impossibility of raising twenty pounds.

'I am so tired of being made to feel guilty all the time. It's about time I got a bit of respect for all the things I *do* do.'

She whipped Cherry's old school cookery apron from a nail on the back of the door and, tying it briskly round her waist, rolled up her sleeves to resume the role of matriarch.

'Aren't you going to introduce your friend, Sean?'

A tall pretty girl was lounging against the sink eating Ryvita out of a packet. She looked less outlandish than most of Sean's friends. There were neat creases down her clean jeans.

'You know Izzie,' mumbled Sean. 'Isobel Weas – . . . Headley-Jones.'

'Of course.' No doubt the recollection of the girl had gone with the demise of a few more brain cells at some point.

'Are you joining us for tea?'

'It's OK, thanks, I've got this Ryvita.'

'Well, sit down all of you anyway.'

She served up the meal which looked sparse enough even without Isobel partaking.

'We had this incredible stroke of luck this afternoon,' said Sean. 'I just ran into Izzie in the town and we went to meet someone at the College and when we were coming through the Walks we found this fifty pence piece and a packet of Ryvita on the bench.'

'I shouldn't have thought you'd want to hang around the College, since you were kicked out,' replied his mother. 'Anyway, you shouldn't have taken it, it's dishonest. That's all there was, just fifty pence?' she added with a very tiny hope.

'Yup.'

'Luke, if you're going to sit there sulking and you don't want that potato, give it to someone who does.' Pearl reached over with her fork and speared a potato from his plate.

In an attempt to fill the silence that followed Isobel remarked, 'It says here that Ryvita is delicious crumbled in milk. Yuk! Have you ever tried it, Mrs Slattery?'

74

'No, I haven't. And you're not about to find out either because we're out of milk.'

The front door bell rang.

'I'll get it.' Cherry beat Tiffany to the door. There was the sound of a male laugh in the hall. Cherry came back, blushing, followed by a young man.

'This is Rick Ruggles. The curate from my church. My mother, brother, sister, various other people.'

Isobel nodded graciously, Luke choked on his orange squash.

'I'm sorry to interrupt your supper. I won't stay.' It was Rick's turn to redden, faced by this battery of eyes.

'It's all right, we've finished. Have a seat.'

At least she didn't say 'Take a pew', thought Cherry as she pushed forward her own chair, everyone else remaining seated.

'Would you like some orange?' offered Pearl. 'You look hot.'

'I'd love some. I'm parched.' He tried to sniff surreptitiously at the damp patch under the arm of his Aertex shirt.

'Mu-um, I hadn't finished that,' wailed Tiffany as Pearl topped up her glass from the tap and handed it to Rick.

'Everybody picks on me just 'cos I'm the youngest.' She looked through lowered lashes at Rick Ruggles.

'Shut up, dear. Off you go and do your homework.'

'Haven't got any.'

'Well, don't then,' Pearl snapped, sitting down heavily, her fingers resisting the itch to reach for the mascara in her pocket.

'I can sympathise. I know what it's like to be the youngest, Stephanie . . .' began Rick jovially.

'Tiffany!'

He felt the wet patches under his arms widen.

'Well, I just called to say that, as you know, Cherry's nobly stepped in to take over one of our Sunday School classes and she's doing a grand job. Poor old Sally who used to do it's had some sort of breakdown, poor lass. I'm just popping over to Netherne to see her now actually. Anyway, we're having a

75

garden party for all the folk who help in the Parish, the Church Family, parents and any other odd bods who care to come along, and I was wondering if you'd like to come, Mrs Slattery. It's at St Elmo's on Saturday and we're all praying the weather will hold out for us.'

'What's Netherne?' said Tiffany.

'Looney bin,' said Sean.

'A garden party. Sounds lovely,' said Pearl weakly, even as the words recalled the dread words Christian House Party to her. She looked at him. He had a kind, if silly, face, and she wondered if there was any point in way-laying him in the hall and telling him that her purse had been stolen, or that she had given her all to the poor, and asking him to lend her twenty pounds. Too late; Cherry was showing him out.

'What do you want to teach in Sunday School for?' Tiffany asked her when she returned. 'I went once, it was dead boring.'

'Because I happen to like children, you little swine.'

She wanted desperately for someone to say something nice about Rick, but no one did. She went upstairs to work.

'Great, isn't it, being invited to a party at my own house by him?' said Luke savagely to Sean.

'The trousers were unfortunate. That limp mottled beige. Wonder where he got them. Perhaps he ran them up himself.'

'Perhaps they were a cry for help.'

'Not to mention the sandals.'

'We used to call them Jesus boots when I was young,' said Pearl.

'Oh shut up! Why do you always have to spoil everything?'

Unfortunately Cherry had chosen that moment to come back into the kitchen.

'You want to watch him, Cherry,' Sean said. 'He fancies you.'

'You're disgusting and you make me sick. All of you!' Cherry screamed. 'I hate you all.'

A little while later Tiffany crept into the room they were

forced to share. Cherry didn't raise her face from the pillow. Tiffany lay down on her own bed and pretended to read a comic.

'Cherry? Cherry?'

'What?' She sat up blotchy-faced with her hair in her eyes.

'You don't hate *me*, do you?'

'Of course I don't hate you, Tiffany. I love you.' Cherry blundered over to Tiffany's bed and embraced her little sister.

'Oh Chri-sorry, you haven't got a tissue have you?'

'I might have.' She searched. 'Here. It's got a little bit of chewing gum in it.'

'Thanks.'

Cherry received the grey rag and wiped her eyes cautiously.

'Anyway,' Tiffany attempted to consolidate her consolation, 'I bet he doesn't fancy you. He's much too old.'

NINE

SNASHFOLD'S was not the ideal environment for a worker with a hangover, or for anyone with the slightest tremor of queasiness. Ivy, the doyenne of the workforce, claimed to be able to diagnose pregnancy before the mother-to-be herself suspected. It was that characteristic nauseous dash to the washroom inspired by the vats of lurid pink and lime green, swirling chocolate, the sickeningly sweet stench of desiccated coconut. The turnover in the predominantly female staff was high.

Barrie, the last, degenerate shoot of the old Snashfold stock, was in a permanent bad temper through worry about money, falling profits, his tax returns, the knowledge that he must institute redundancies, and that even if he did so, he must eventually close. He had an ulcer, which he bathed constantly in condensed milk, eaten with a spoon from the tin, and spent much of his time in the betting shop. When he returned to the factory he usually managed to reduce one of the girls to tears. Now he was being persecuted by some nerd who claimed to be writing a book on Redhill in Bygone Days. 'Gordon Bennett, who wants another book on bleedin' Redhill?' he protested in vain. This guy was forever harassing him for photos of the factory in its heyday; of the bearded patriarch standing by the stone fountain surrounded by his smiling workforce in snowy caps and aprons. Barrie pondered gloomily the result of the publication of such photographs in the *Surrey Mirror*; the crashingly dull reminiscences of octogenarians, the pleas to trace long-lost relatives, the unsolicited letters that would gather dust like the leaves and sweet-papers that choked the dry mouth of the broken fountain. He took a black refuse sack and crammed into it pictures, letters, photographs, albums and dumped the lot in the dustbin.

'There's nothing left, nothing,' he told the would-be historian. 'It was all destroyed in the war. Another little bit of our heritage gone. Tragic, innit?'

He bared his yellow teeth in a scummy smile and licked a shred of tobacco from his lip.

The kid who came whingeing round about a school project was punished with a bar of Snashfold's Jawbreaker, a sort of edible alternative to the thick ear Barrie would have liked to give him.

'Mr Barrie, do you think we could have a word? Some of the girls are getting very worried and . . .'

'I'm in a meeting,' he said firmly, shutting the door of his little office on them and locking it. He plunged his sticky spoon into the jagged mouth of the tin and, closing his eyes, gave himself up to sweet white oblivion.

'Last in, first out,' was the consensus. Pearl felt that her position was perilous, especially so since she had spotted young Tracey teetering out of Busby's on Mr Barrie's arm. She wondered if she had made a mistake in repulsing his advances when she started at Snashfold's. Well, it was too late now, she reflected, as she scooped a heap of sweets into her handbag.

'What's happening about that inquiry?' she asked Ida.

'The plaster?'

'No, I meant the nail-file.'

'Dunno. It's still *sub judice*.'

'Whose do you reckon it was? I know it wasn't mine, I haven't got one.'

'You mean you haven't got one now,' someone put in unkindly from further down the line. The uncertainty was turning Sister against Sister.

'My money's on young Tracey,' said Ida diplomatically and the workforce was for a moment reunited. Tracey, returning from one of her frequent trips to the toilet, caught her name and went as red as a peardrop, clamping her thin lips as on a taste of acid.

Ivy explained to Pearl the meaning of workers' co-operative.

'I don't suppose anyone would like to lend me twenty quid?' asked Pearl hopelessly.

The answering silence was drowned by the clatter of archaic machinery.

'There's your boyfriend,' said Ida later as they crossed the car park together after work. Malcolm was hulking nonchalantly under the abused lime tree.

'He's not . . .' Pearl started to say. She had toyed with the idea of constructing a small placard, to be held up behind Malcolm's head, which would read: 'This man is not my Boyfriend.'

'Like a lift home? I was just passing . . .'

'Ida?' Pearl turned to her, but she was already buckling on a helmet.

'No, ta, I've got my bike,' she said, slithering into a pair of protective nylon trousers.

'Do you want to go straight home or have you got any shopping to do?' Malcolm asked as the Cortina snouted into the traffic.

Pearl hesitated. Malcolm could often be relied on to insist on picking up the tab at the checkout, ignoring her weak protests, but tonight she had, as it were, other fish to fry.

'No, it's OK thanks. If you could just stop at the chippie, I'll get some chips for tea.'

'You sit there, you look tired. I'll get them,' said Malcolm, pulling up outside the Conger Fish Palace.

'No, no, put it away,' he added as Pearl opened her handbag.

'Don't be daft. Why on earth should you pay for our tea?' she protested, leaning back and lighting a cigarette.

She wound down her window and called after him, 'Get some pickled eggs. And a couple of gherkins. Big ones.'

'Can you slow down a minute? I want to look at that house.' They were turning into Woodlands Road, the chips hot in Pearl's lap, the car filling tantalisingly with the scent of warm paper and vinegar. There was one house in the Slatterys' street which had not fallen into decay, and outside which Pearl and Malcolm now sat in the car.

'*Et in Arcadio ego . . .*' murmured Malcolm.

'What?'

The name of the house, Arcadia, floated in faded gold letters on a clear glass oblong above the door; on each side a white stork in green glass reeds stabbed its slender gold beak towards a central panel of sesame and lilies. The occupants were two elderly ladies; sometimes when working in their front garden, one, say, cutting the hedge and the other sweeping up the clippings, in their gardening aprons with pockets for trowels and secateurs, they would raise a hessian glove in acknowledgment of Pearl as she passed. It seemed to her that they had got everything right. She knew without entering the house, and she would never be invited in, that it would be just so; there would be no fuss or hassle. Each week would have its pattern and each day its appointed tasks so that their year would unroll like a calm illustrated calendar, and the house would smell of beeswax and pot-pourri from their own roses, in whose perfect scented intricacies no earwig dared lurk. Sometimes, returning from a Sunday morning trip to the newsagent's for a paper or cigarettes, Pearl would encounter them, in their hats, coming home from church, and drew sometimes comfort, sometimes pain, from the knowledge that their lunch would be sizzling quietly in the oven while they each sipped a single shimmering cut-glass thistle of sherry and discussed the sermon.

'OK, you can drive on now, thanks.'

'Why do you always stare at that house? I've noticed before.'

'Oh – no reason, really.'

Pearl did not want to discuss, and couldn't explain, her fascination by, and envy of the occupants of Arcadia. She wanted to be those two ladies.

'Are you busy later?' asked Malcolm as he pulled up outside her house. 'I thought perhaps we might do something . . .'

'Yes, no doubt we will,' Pearl thought. Aloud, she said, 'You can call for me later if you like.'

She got out of the car, with the chips, leaving Malcolm to drive away to get his own supper.

'Do you really have to have ketchup and vinegar and salad cream on your chips, Tiffany?'

Pearl shuddered at the lurid sunset spreading over her daughter's plate. 'No, don't answer,' she added hastily as Tiffany prepared to open her mouth.

Luke pushed his plate away. Three pairs of hands shot out. Cherry, at the far end of the table, aloof from the rest of the group, in spirit as well as having the distinction of a knife and fork, lifted her head from one of the glossy brochures piled beside her plate.

'D'you want to look at my prospectuses?' she said, handing one to her mother. Pearl gazed bleakly at a photograph of a smiling girl in a short Shetland wool jumper and tight brown trousers, apparently engaging in banter with a giant three-dimensional model of the structure of DNA. She feared that she would be called upon to fill in forms.

'You know you can't wear Shetland,' she said at last. 'It gives you a rash.' A pale red wash like paint water into which a brush has been dipped just once ran over Cherry's face as she snatched back the booklet. Luke thought he saw a light go out behind her eyes. He almost hated Pearl. He must be mad, or perverse, to love such a woman, he thought.

'Can I have a look, please?' he said, reaching for the prospectus, but Sean had grabbed it.

'Brown cords,' was his comment.

'And she's got a fat stomach,' added Tiffany over his shoulder. 'What's it for, Cher, are they catalogues?'

But Cherry and the prospectuses were leaving the kitchen and the door slammed behind them, causing the oven door to crash open, in shock, or sympathy. Sean and Tiffany shrugged and divided between them the tiny cold squares of chip butty congealing on Cherry's plate. Pearl rose to slam the oven door on the brown greasy cavern within.

'The twenty quid will sort things out,' she was thinking as Luke surveyed with animosity her hips swelling like a blue melon as she crouched to pick up an old burnt chip from the floor.

'Get this mess cleared up.' She waved a hand at the remains of their meal, inadvertently placing the ancient chip in her mouth and grimacing as she spat out the fluff from the floor, which had adhered. 'I'm going to have a bath and woe betide anyone who hasn't cleaned it! Or used up the bubble bath.'

'Only teachers say "woe betide",' Tiffany remarked, but only when Pearl's steps were heard on the stairs.

'How would you know?' Sean and Luke spoke simultaneously.

'Jinx,' said Tiffany unperturbedly, 'shake little fingers,' running her finger round her plate and licking salad cream from it.

'You heard what Mum said,' Sean told her. 'Wash up.'

'She didn't say me.'

'I'll do it,' said Luke. He could not face another squabble and started stacking the dishes miserably. Sean and Tiffany left him to it. Behind him, from the television which had been on, unregarded, throughout the meal the theme from 'Cross-roads' unrolled its melancholy boom. Only a trickle came from the hot tap, the main flow being diverted into Pearl's

bath, and he had to prise off the cap of the washing-up liquid
bottle and fill it with cold water before he could get any sort of
suds. He was thinking about Cherry's face. OK, so she was
snooty to him, and resented his having her room, and had
become unbearably smug since she had been Saved and had
deserted to the Ruggles camp, but still he felt her disappointment and frustration at her family's reception of the prospectuses. Half-way through his task, he wiped his hands on his
jeans and went to find her, intending to say something en-
couraging; but when he opened Tiffany's door he saw Sean
sitting beside Cherry on the bed, one arm round her shoulder,
a cigarette trailing from the fingers of the other hand, their
heads, one blonde, the other turned orange overnight,
together.

'What about Cardiff then?' Sean was saying.

Neither of them looked up.

'What the hell am I doing here?' Luke muttered savagely, back
at the sink. 'I don't belong here. I don't belong anywhere.'

He scrubbed, through a blur of tears, at the sediment under
the rack on the draining board with an old piece of Brillo pad
like a tangled hank of hair from a long-dead horse, then had a
go at the taps. He didn't want the job to be finished; he had
absolutely nothing else to do.

'What the hell do you think you're doing?'

Pearl stood blazing at him.

'I was just scouring the inside of the teapot . . .'

He stood, the teapot dangling from his hand.

'Give it here. If I wanted the bloody teapot scoured, I'd do it
myself. How dare you!'

She snatched it from him and caught him a blow across the
arm.

'Don't you see how insulting it is?!' She crashed the teapot
down and seized him by both shoulders and shook him.

'Well, don't you?'

Luke's head nodded violently in submission as she shook,
then suddenly let go. Luke leant dumbly against the sink.

'What's up with you?' Cherry came into the kitchen. 'You look a bit . . . shaken.'

Pearl laughed. Luke managed a watery grin.

'He is,' she said. 'I'm sorry, Luke. But you do see, don't you?'

'I'm sorry too,' said Luke.

He could not know that Pearl's rage was inspired mostly by thought of the evening with Malcolm. There was a double ring of the doorbell.

'Oh God, there's Malcolm. I wish he wouldn't always ring like that . . . make sure Tiffany goes to bed at a reasonable hour . . . bye.'

After his rough treatment, Luke felt restless. He drifted into the garden, batting with his fist a dry dress of Pearl's that had been baking on the washing line for days and dislodging an earwig from its bodice. He shuddered; it was too graveyard an image. Attracted by a clunking sound he went over to the fence; the larger of the two male tortoises was on its hind legs astride the shell of its companion; it reared backwards and then bashed down, stretching wide its mouth and emitting a squeak from its pink interior. Luke was dumbfounded; he had supposed tortoises to be entirely dumb. The smaller tortoise struggled free and made off at a fast pace to the shelter of a bushy foxglove, giving the lie, too, to the notion that tortoises are slow, pursued by the rapacious reptile, who being solar-powered, would not desist until the heat had gone out of the sun. Leaning over the balcony of one of the flats in the block of ill-repute, a woman eased her shoulder straps; the brilliant white strips of flesh against the violent pink suggested that she would be *hors de combat* that night.

Pearl's manhandling of him, the tortoises, the sunburned woman, all compounded Luke's restlessness. He went and lay on his bed.

All these people snouting and nuzzling at her; she might as well get something out of it. Pearl remembered a television serial she had watched years ago; 'Nana', it was called. She was a courtesan; she had the right idea; she rode around in carriages and wore beautiful clothes; she sang 'I'm Venus, blonde Venus, the Goddess of Love' and had all Paris at her feet, while Pearl was having it away in a room above a pub in Redhill. She groaned aloud.

'Darling.'

Malcolm's tongue was like a slug in her ear. It was as much as she could do not to scream and push him away. From the tracks a train hooted like a lonesome whip-poor-will. She saw herself running after it and leaping aboard, to be carried away. She clenched her fists so that they could not thump Malcolm's head; she was drenched in his sweat. She concentrated on his dressing-table; a tin of talc stood in a mist of its own powder on the splitting thin wood surface. Malcolm, talcum. She watched the red numerals flicker on his clock radio and wondered if she could reach with her toe to switch on some music.

A few minutes later she found herself twisting the wet ginger fur on his back into little peaks, in a gesture of true tenderness. Malcolm sucked two cigarettes from the pack and lit them with a single flourish of his Zippo lighter. An acrid, unmistakable stench of burning filter-tip hit the air. He spat them out.

'Cut the tips off, that's what I do when I light the wrong end,' said Pearl. Modestly girdling himself in the sheet Malcolm hobbled to the dressing-table and returned with a pair of scissors whose blades curved alarmingly like those used to cut toenails.

'Bastard,' said Pearl.

'What?' he almost dropped his sheet.

'Not you. Jack.'

'Divorce him.'

'I can't.'

'Why not?'

'I'm not married to him.'

She inhaled on her snipped cigarette which tasted faintly of melted cellulose. The end of Nana had been a bit of a downer, she remembered. Cio-Cio-San was scratching at the door.

'Thank you, Pearl,' said Malcolm. 'It's been a long time.'

'Too long,' she lied, cheered by the thought of the three brown ten pound notes, euphemistically borrowed, in her handbag.

TEN

'YOU know you don't really want to come.'

'Of course I do, if you want me to.'

'Of course I want you to. It's just so awkward to get to, and Rick's car's only a two-seater. And you wouldn't know anybody . . .'

'I'd know you. And Rick. Sort of. Anyway I suppose everybody else's parents will be there . . .'

Pearl and Cherry stared at each other, caught in deadlock, neither knowing what the other really wanted.

'Anyway, I'm coming. I've decided, so that's settled.'

'Great. Thanks, Mum.'

Pearl didn't allow herself to notice a faint look of conscious kindness on Cherry's face.

'Have you seen my white blouse?'

'It's in the airing cupboard,' said Pearl, pleased to have done something right at last. Then she remembered that it had come back pink from the wash.

A light shower which had fallen earlier in the afternoon had left Redhill station in a state of flood. The roof dripped, a cascade of black water sluiced the steps and gathered in muddy lakes, the iron handrail was cold and slimy. As Pearl picked her way through the puddles on the platform she felt a cold wind whip the skirt of her cotton dress round her bare legs and mud ooze between her toes. A small diesel train throbbed at platform one and at intervals announcements in Welsh crackled through the loudspeaker system suspended above the empty platforms. A conveyer belt hung with hooks for suspending mailsacks rattled in an endless loop, combining with the smell of burning oil, the pointless announcements and the drilling engine to give her a headache. There were heaps of grey and brown mailsacks, slumped on trolleys, waiting for collection, and as she ran her fingers along the stitching Pearl's feeling of desolation intensified and gooseflesh rose on her arms as she touched the wet grey plastic and sodden canvas and the cold metal rings sewn by captive fingers. At last the train left platform one leaving her to the sound of dripping and the jangling hooks. She was sure that her train should have arrived long ago, but there was no announcement concerning it, no one to ask and the clock had two pieces of sticking plaster criss-crossing its face. A Brighton train arrived at platform three, and departed. She walked to the end of the platform and stared at a house standing in a waste garden of dross, the last one of a demolished terrace which the occupants had refused to leave. Pearl had read about them in the *Surrey Mirror*. Smoke was coming from the chimney and Pearl wondered what they were doing in their brick shell, marooned in rubble under their damp spiral of smoke. At last a train arrived and Pearl got on, hoping it stopped at Purley. It did not and she had to go on to East Croydon and change. Having come thus far on what seemed more and more of a fool's errand she would not turn back, but by the time she found St Elmo's Vicarage her feet and legs were purple and her lips were blue, and she acknowledged that Cherry had not wanted her to come, and she had not wanted to go.

A man in a beige windcheater zipped against the wind and a knitted hat sat at a folding table in the gateway with a beige spool of raffle tickets and a Tupperware box half-full of money. A sign said 'Entrance 50p'.

'Shame about the weather,' he sympathised, taking in her limp dress.

'I don't know, makes a nice change not to be too hot.'

'Have you got a ticket or did you want to buy one?'

Pearl stared at him for a moment. 'In my bag,' she said, firmly, patting that tatty reticule, and leaving the gravel she strode as purposefully as her shoes would allow across the wet grass.

'Well, really!' she said to the first person she encountered. 'That's the first party I've been invited to where you have to pay to get in.' As she spoke she realised that it was the first party of any kind she had been asked to for a long time.

'It's all in a good cause,' bleated her new acquaintance.

'Huh.' She peeped into her companion's paper cup and saw a residue of foamy orange and a pineapple cube. A horrible fear possessed her.

'What else –' she started to say, but found herself deserted. The red and white spotted dress had looked so chic in the mail-order catalogue, but now she stood, an uncertain toadstool in the soaking grass, not knowing which way to turn and remembering the latest threatening letter concerning payment which rested in a mess of eggshells and tealeaves in the bin under the sink. Groups of people in sweaters and anoraks broke as they passed her and resumed their laughing conversations. She envied them their sensible shoes and warm socks as they walked over the erratic swathes of green, where Rick had seized the mower from old Boxall, and given up the attempt to civilise the garden; laurels and rhododendrons prevailed; the roses were cabbagey and corrupt and a few faint foxgloves struggled in the borders. A pall of burning meat hung over one end of the garden. Rick held out his blistered palms to the fire, the centre of a circle of laughing youngsters.

'I say, Cherry, look, isn't that your mother? Over there by the yew, all by herself. I'll go and bring her over.' Rick bounded up to her.

'Hello, Mrs S. So glad you could make it. Let me get you a drink and introduce you to some folk.'

Pearl brightened. 'What've you got?' She shivered. 'I could really fancy a drop of ruby port. It's that sort of weather, isn't it?'

'Ha ha ha, yes indeed. Tea or squash, take your pick, or can I recommend the Ruggles special, it's my own concoction, with a secret ingredient.'

They approached a trestle table, near the barbecue.

'The Ruggles special,' she repeated.

'That's the spirit!' Unfortunately, thought Pearl, it was not, as she sipped at the ladleful of pale liquid sloshed into her paper cup and tried to avoid a piece of apple peel.

'Is the grass the secret ingredient?' She fished out a blade and smeared it on the side of her cup.

'Mother!'

'I'm sorry.' Rick blushed. 'It does get everywhere, doesn't it?'

Pearl soon felt superfluous among Cherry's friends and stood slightly apart watching a farrow of sausages rolling and spitting on the grid. She edged nearer the flames but was repelled by the smell of the fat which hung in melting cones and stalactites. Pearl saw the man who had asked for her ticket approaching, and moved away. Children ran about flinging handfuls of grass at each other, rubbing it in each other's hair and on their clothes. Pearl felt lost, bereft of her own children and wished that there was a small hand in her own to anchor her, although Cherry was only a few yards away. She almost mourned her children. Her feet were numb; she didn't dare look at her legs as she walked aimlessly about. She came across two wheelchairs stuck in the middle of the lawn, their occupants stranded in a sea of grass. The marooned pair sat staring straight in front of them.

'Would you like me to push . . . ?' began Pearl.

'Push off,' said one of them. Wounded, repulsed, feeling as much part of the party as a wormcast on the lawn, she lurched off. Where were those folk Rick had promised to introduce her to?

'Hello, you look a bit lost. Do you know many folk here? There's going to be singing and dancing later.'

91

A little woman, neat as a kindly skittle, materialised. Pearl shook her head.

'One of those boys was just very rude to me.' She spoke without meaning to, needing to share her hurt.

'Bless them,' said her rescuer absently. 'Come and have some fruit cup. We call it Rick's special.'

The ladle clashed in the enamel bowl.

'There. I've managed to capture you a piece of orange. I haven't seen you in church, have I?'

'No, I . . .'

'It's always nice to see a new face.'

'I'm Cherry's mother.'

'Of course you are,' she said, reassuringly. 'I must get some folk to come and say hello. Brian!' she called.

A youth galloped up. 'This is Cherry's mother. She doesn't know anybody. Do you think you could get her a sausage or something? Good lad.' She clapped him on the shoulder and turned to Pearl. 'You look half-frozen, my dear. I've got a spare cardi in my bag, I'll just fetch it.'

'Please, don't bother, I –' Pearl tried to recall her through blue lips. A shred of orange was caught between her front teeth.

'How do you like the Ruggles special?' asked Brian. His own lips were thick and rosy, his neck rose flushed and warm from a creamy Aran sweater. A sausage which he had hitherto concealed split its skin as he bit into it and a piece of gristle flew on to Pearl's face.

'Oh, sorry!'

'It's OK. What do you do?' She couldn't afford to let him escape; he was all she had.

'I'm one of the vast army of the Unemployed,' he grinned ruefully, revealing big white healthy teeth. 'No, seriously, I'm filling in a year before going up to university so I'm spending the time helping Rick with his youth counselling.'

'Oh.' She did not ask what qualifications he had for counselling anybody.

'How about you?'

'I work in a sweet factory. In Redhill.'

'Not old Snashfold's? I went for a holiday job there once, but I couldn't stick the smell. Bit of a dump, isn't it?'

In reply Pearl poured what was left of her drink on to the grass.

'You'd think they'd run to something a bit better, wouldn't you, at fifty pence a throw? I bet they've got barrels of wine in the vestry.' They glared at each other, he unaware that he had said anything offensive. Simultaneously they started to walk away from each other and so found that they were walking together. Pearl stumbled on a tussock and grabbed his arm, attracting some glances.

'Ah!' Rick Ruggles threw out a welcoming arm, embracing the air. 'This is our Cherry's mum,' he said to the two women with him.

'*My* Cherry,' thought Pearl, 'or at least she was.' She tried to smile at them but her lip wobbled and it was all she could do to stop her chin from puckering.

'Have you been admiring the project Cherry's done with the Toddlers' Group?'

Pearl shook her head. It was the first she had heard of it.

'Oh you must, it's over there on the display table. What a pretty frock, but aren't you frozen? My husband's got an old golfing anorak in the back of the car. I'll send someone to fetch it for you.'

Feeling like a large foolish exhibit herself she shook her head again.

'Such a shame about the weather, when it's been so lovely.'

'Maybe Someone up there doesn't like you,' said Pearl. It came out too harshly to pass for a joke. They all looked up at the sky as if her words flapped there like large unpleasant crows. She racked her brains for something pleasant to say. 'I like your brooch.' She indicated the small silver object on the other's sweater.

'Oh, thank you. Actually it's an ichthys.'

'Oh, I thought it was a fish.'

Ruggles coughed.

'Excuse me, I want to find my daughter.' '*My* daughter,' Pearl muttered to herself as she went to find a hiding place to smoke the cigarette she craved, 'whom you've stolen from me and made despise me,' having realised almost on entering the garden that no one else was smoking. She struck off towards a group of trees, beyond caring as they watched her leave the throng and almost colliding with a person in a sort of black nun's habit carrying a tray of sausage rolls. Baby nettles caressed her bare legs as she cracked through the undergrowth to the safety of a steaming compost heap under a dancing cloud of midges. It was quite dry beneath the trees. She drew greedily on the cigarette, leaning against a yew trunk which brushed black smudges on to her arms and the back of her dress.

'What am I doing here? I should never have come, I've got to get out.' She tossed down the half-smoked cigarette and was about to grind it with her foot.

'Good God, woman, are you trying to set the place on fire? The Reverend Ichabod Ribbons, sausage roll in hand, stood watching her.

'Oh, go to hell,' said Pearl, starting to walk away.

'No, don't go,' he said, brushing crumbs from his silvery shirt front. 'You look frozen.'

'I hope you're not going to offer me a cardigan or anorak.'

'No.' He patted the pocket of his own jacket and pulled out a silver flask.

'Have a drop of this. Warm you up.'

She unscrewed the flask and put it to her lips.

'Steady on, I said a drop.'

'That hit the spot!' said Pearl, smiling and handing it back. 'Ta very much. Beats the Ruggles special.'

'What's that?' He shook the last few drops into his mouth and wiped it with the back of his hand.

'Any sign of people going yet?' he asked gloomily.

'Doesn't look like it.'

The strains of a guitar and a high clear female voice singing 'Amazing Grace' came through the trees.

'Ah well,' he said and stumped off exhaling nicotine and brandy.

Feeling much more cheerful, Pearl emerged from the wood brushing a dead catkin from her hair.

'Got any peppermints or chewing gum, love?' she asked Cherry who shook her head fiercely and turned away.

'I've got a Double Amplex.' Someone shook a little white box of pills at her.

'Thanks.' Pearl did not know if she was being insulting or was simply an Amplex addict who had to carry a fix with her to feed her habit, as she popped two little yellow balls into her own mouth.

'Anyone got a train timetable?' asked Pearl as there was a sudden sizzle on the grid and at once glass tear drops, pear drops, assaulted them with such violence, turning to hailstones that the people, as one, gathered up things and children and ran for the Vicarage.

A prolonged banging on the back door at last produced the rattling of a bolt and chains and the Vicar appeared.

'Ah, good people, come in, come in.'

He drew back his lips in a smile before he was pressed back by the surge. The kitchen filled with the smell of wet wool. He felt that something was expected of him. He raised his hand in what could have been a benediction and let it fall. 'Dearly beloved . . .' he might have been about to say. Rick pushed up the window and slammed it on a curlicue of ivy which catapulted a volley of small white shot on to the remains of Mr Ribbons's unsociable supper; a sliver of pink meat adhering to a glossy stucco crust and a hoop of bluish egg. The sound of engines revving and the whirr of wheels on gravel indicated that some guests had taken to their cars. Pearl found herself pressed up against Rick Ruggles, in dangerous proximity to an armpit, as people jostled for the chairs and perched on the table's edge; the younger folk arranged themselves in youthful attitudes on the windowsills. The Deaconess was struggling with an urn of boiling water, to the peril of those close to the stove, and looking round in vain for empty cups, a panicky moustache of moisture on her upper lip.

'I don't suppose you've got a train timetable?' Pearl asked the Vicar, hoping that he might proffer a quick snort over its pages in the privacy of another room.

'There's a Bradshaw in my study.'

Before they could fight their way to its obsolete charms a tentative hand fluttered on Pearl's arm and a voice said, 'I'll run you home.'

'How kind. It's Redhill.'

She looked up into a waxy face with colourless hair which spoke of years of dysentery in the mission field.

'Shall we go?'

He steered her through the steaming bodies.

'Night all.'

The Vicar's brandy had not quite lost its effect.

'Still pissing down,' remarked Pearl as they surveyed the spitting gravel. 'Reminds me of the seaside. God, it must be years since I went to Brighton.' She added wistfully, 'D'you ever go there?'

'I spent a couple of days at a convention in Hove recently.'

'Figures . . .' muttered Pearl.

'You'd better take my jacket.'

He placed the large tweed garment round her shoulders, exposing his gaunt corded arms and Aertex shirt, veterans of many monsoons, to the Surrey storm. Pearl slipped her arms gratefully into the sleeves, the silk lining caressed her arms.

After a confusion of seat belts she found herself bowling along, securely buckled in a little grey Morris Minor, through the rain. They passed two wheelchairs, the drivers' heads darkened by and bent against the rain, lumbering along the flooded pavement, silver daggers of water flashing from their laborious tyres.

'Cigarette?'

'Not for me thanks, you go ahead.'

She couldn't see an ashtray and had to wind down the

window to flick her ash; a flurry of rain hit her face and a large drop sizzled on the cigarette, threatening to extinguish it.

'I used to smoke,' he said, 'until I realised that I should be spending God's money on other things.'

'Oh.'

There seemed little to say after that. Pearl became aware of a slight disturbance on his seat, and lowering her eyes saw a palsied quivering of the beige-clad thigh nearest her. He was trembling like a medieval monk whose cell has been visited by the devil in the guise of a temptress. She shifted discreetly to her left, slightly alarmed but with a secret smirk of satisfaction that this prig was not immune to her powers.

'What do you do, for a living, I mean?' she asked.

'Well, after my last bout of malaria . . .' he began.

'Malaria!' she interrupted. 'Don't you have to drink gin for that? The quinine . . .' The lights of a pub sizzled invitingly in the windscreen.

'Tonic water,' he said with a dry laugh as the lights were extinguished by the rain.

'Next left,' said Pearl flatly. Whatever effervescence there had been between them evaporated like the bubbles in a stale drink as the car drew up outside the Slatterys' house scrunching over a can in the gutter. She heard the familiar sound of splitting stitches as she slid from the car.

'Thanks for the lift.'

She backed away and waited for him to pull out before hobbling up the steps, his jacket pulled tight over the back of her skirt.

'Thank God to be home.' She expelled a huge sigh as she entered her own kitchen, but there sat Ruggles and Cherry wreathed in the innocuous steam of two mugs of coffee.

'Well, I think that went off very well,' said Pearl brightly. 'Shame about the weather though.'

They took in her mud-spattered legs, the torn skirt, the borrowed man's jacket.

She saw Luke slumped sulkily in the corner examining a small blister on his foot.

'Stop picking your feet!' she said sharply.

'I wasn't,' he began indignantly. 'I was just . . .'

But she turned away and shook the empty milk bottle indignantly and he was left scowling miserably, branded a slob now in addition to everything else.

'I'm going for a walk.'

Pearl swept out of the kitchen. Luke slunk after her, a hopeless whipped dog, beyond being shamed by the glance that passed between Ruggles and Cherry.

'Christ, what an evening,' Pearl said savagely in the hall.

'Don't suppose you've got any money, Luke? Hey, what's this?' She drew out of the jacket pocket a five pound note, several ones, and a handful of silver glittering in the broken light of the chandelier. An almost lascivious smile spread across her face as she tucked her arm through Luke's.

'Come on, we've got at least half an hour.'

The stab of her heel on his bare foot was a blissful agony as she pulled him through the door.

'First Malcolm,' thought Pearl, 'now this little windfall.' And the jacket wasn't bad. It seemed that the wages of sin were quite good after all.

'Every cloud has a silver lining,' she remarked, as she led Luke in the opposite direction from that of Malcolm's pub, the pavement warm and not unpleasantly gritty beneath his soles, and dismissed Malcolm entirely from her mind as they homed in through the deafening music on a corner seat in the Wheatsheaf and she settled herself on the orange upholstery and dispatched Luke to the bar to fight his way through the Saturday crowd.

'I had a drink with a vicar tonight,' she told Luke on his return with the glasses.

'Hey, I suppose he was your father?'

'So I've always been led to believe,' he said stiffly.

'He seemed a sweet bloke. About the only semi-human person there. Why don't you get on with him?'

'Huh.'

Across the room a man slurped the last glob from a tub of

98

jellied eels and raised the polystyrene tub in salute to Pearl. She responded with her glass, already decorated with half a lipstick smile. Luke glared at him and drank deeply. Inch by inch, if that was the correct mode of measurement, he had felt his personality disappear since he had brought what was left of him to the Slatterys'.

Apart from almost total neglect by his father, Luke had often suffered a lash of pure dislike from his cloudy eyes. The fact of his existence was a mystery to him; he assumed that his had not been an immaculate conception or a virgin birth and could surmise only that his father, inflamed by overindulgence at some Harvest Supper, had forced his attentions on a wife too sozzled on sherry trifle to resist. However, it was not a picture on which he cared to dwell for long. As he sat opposite Pearl in what should have been such happiness but which had been wrecked by the mention of his father, he was forced to recall their penultimate meeting, in the courtroom when he had been sent down.

The magistrate was pronouncing sentence. Luke stared at the old buffoon in total disbelief. Where was the fatherly twinkle in the fishy eye, the just-concealed tremor of amusement behind the harsh metallic fringe that barricaded the upper lip?

'You don't understand . . . I . . .'

'I understand only too well.'

It seemed that Luke was all the more culpable because he was the son of a clergyman, and now here was his progenitor bursting into the back of the courtroom like a well-filled decanter exuding fumes of sherry, brushing cake crumbs from his stomach, and blustering something about being held up at a funeral, but Luke was already being prodded towards the cells. It was unbelievable. He was not the sort of person who was punished. He was the one who always charmed his way out of trouble. Almost immediately a circlet of spots burst through his skin and shone in jewels of shame on his chin.

'What about your father?' he asked Pearl now, to divert his thoughts from his own.

'What about him? I haven't seen him for years.'

They had kept in touch in a desultory fashion but at each meeting there had been less to say; each had felt the inexplicable details and the circumstances of his and her life mass like a silent unscalable wall between them and they fell silent until at last they were able only to push towards each other the stained sugar or clogged ketchup tomato across the cheap café table top. Then, two years ago, she had been sitting in a train at Clapham Junction, bound for Victoria, observing dispassionately the strange sub-species trainspotter, when she had spotted a once-familiar figure clad in ill-cut jeans and anorak, the hood's drawstring pulled tight round the face, a pair of binoculars slung round the neck. She was close enough to see the beetroot in his bitten sandwich, the thick white bread incarnadined, the moving lump in the jaw, remembered with a jolt, as he chewed. He raised the sandwich in a vague salute to his daughter then swung round on his built-up heel as a train approached the opposite platform, addressing himself to the more important matter of a suburban engine number.

'He's a trainspotter,' Pearl shouted to Luke.

'Why?' He leaned towards her to catch her answer.

'Why not?' Her tone was suddenly belligerent, the alcohol inspiring a respect she did not feel for her, apparently, slighted sire.

'Well, you see all these nerds in flares and anoraks with notebooks in the snow on Clapham station . . .'

'My glass would appear to be empty,' she replied ominously, pushing some money in a wet trail across the table. Luke was affected differently. At the bar, he felt the gin he had drunk burst in an opalescent rainbow of happiness in his chest. He tapped his fingers on the bar to the beat of the music, his elbow in a puddle of beer as he waited to be served. Suddenly he saw the future as clear and simple in the lucid colour of gin, almost a perspex palace that was his for the entering; anxiety fell from him like a scaly suit; he felt it slither from his skin to the floor. He caught sight of a pretty face in the mirror behind the bar and smiled; the face smiled back and he saw that it was his. The girl serving him smiled and he felt some power, a golden aura that had tarnished at his arrest, and quite disappeared by the time of his appearance in the courtroom, return. The little blue bottle winked like a cobalt jewel in his mind.

'God's money,' Pearl snorted. She felt deeply weary as she stretched out her legs and surveyed her feet; the mud had dried round her nails and between her toes. She glared at a youth in leathers, one leg in a plaster cast stretched stiffly and perilously out in front of him, his metal sticks a hazard to all. He winked at her, the badges which studded his leather jacket all winked in a dazzling breastplate as he lifted his glass. Talk about stupid, as if God couldn't make any amount of money He wanted, if He could be bothered. A dull ache, like incipient toothache, hinted that her visit to the garden party had been a disaster and that she would pay for it. A hen party at a large circular table was getting loud; there was a dangerous edge to the laughter. Two of the girls pushed back their chairs and started to dance, joining a pair of punks whose emerald and sapphire crests bobbed like a pair of macaws in the smoke in the narrow space between two tables. When Luke returned at last he found the youth in leathers sitting at their table and an enormous bare foot protruding from a plaster cast on his chair. He settled himself back in his chair, lit a cigarette and blew the smoke in a thin vicious stream into Luke's face as he stood by the table. A dotted line, marked CUT, circled the base at his throat, and the name Lemmy was tattooed on his right hand.

'Have you got a pen?' Luke asked Pearl.

She scrabbled in her bag and came up with an orange felt-tip.

'May I?'

Lemmy gave an imperceptible nod.

With a flourish, Luke bent over the outstretched leg and inscribed 'Piss Off' in orange on the virgin cast.

The youth knew he was beaten. He clanked back to his own table, where he sat scowling. 'I'll get you,' he muttered from time to time. He had a swastika made from rear-light reflectors on the back of his jacket and its red facets flashed as they caught the light when he moved. A skull on his hand scowled when he clenched his fist.

The clucks and squawks from the hen party grew wilder; barnyard noises hanging in the smoky air.

'"Vaudeville lays an egg in Schenectady,"' said Pearl.

'What?'

'I dunno – I just felt like saying it.'

'Why? What does it mean?'

'Oh – don't be so boring. I don't know . . .'

'It means, Herr Fassbinder, that the lady, for reasons best known to herself, is quoting from *Babes in Arms*, starring Judy Garland and Mickey Rooney . . .'

'Tone!' Luke choked on his drink as he and Pearl swivelled round at the male voice that crumbled like rich fruit cake in its owner's throat. The taxi driver who had driven him to Pearl's house on his arrival in Redhill gave a little bow to Pearl.

'Anthony Troop,' he said. 'Mind if I join you?' He pronounced the 'h' in his name. His smile flashed gold, and he wore a gold ingot, on a chain round his neck.

'Your English is coming along nicely,' he said to Luke. 'You could do with a bit of work on your accent though . . .'

'*Ja*,' bleated Luke, his eyes transfixed by Tone's gold-thewed thighs flexing in rather threatening jogging shorts.

'What's going on? What's he talking about, Luke?'

'Luke, is it?' Tone leered at him.

'Well, Luke, I wouldn't say no to a Tequila Sunrise . . .' He sighed heavily at the gibbering boy and pulled a roll of notes from his shorts pocket and peeled off a blue one. 'Same again?' he asked Pearl.

Luke didn't have to wait for her answer; he set off for the bar, his legs heavy, as in a nightmare and Tone settled himself in his vacated seat.

'My son's got a pair of shorts like those,' Pearl was saying as he fought his way round the hen party.

'Him?'

Luke felt Tone's head jerk towards his back.

'No, he's not mine. Elvis, my oldest boy.' As he retreated from the image of Elvis's oiled and glistening thighs filling the thin grey cotton jersey, his own bare feet felt spindly and vulnerable. A boot's edge chipped his little toe. When he returned Tone was flipping a Marlboro from a soft pack towards Pearl and lighting it for her.

'No,' he was saying, filtering smoke from his own cigarette through narrowed nostrils. 'I gave our young friend a free ride in my cab on the understanding that he would reimburse me the following evening. Haven't seen hide nor hair of him since, till now, that is.' Luke, the hairs on his shivering hide standing up in fear, set the drinks down on the table.

'Clumsy.' Tone mopped the table with a tissue. 'You are a mucky pup aren't you? For reasons best known to himself,' he continued, to Pearl, and to the interest of Lemmy, who shifted his cast closer to listen, 'he was impersonating a German student. Said he'd been mugged at East Croydon, lost his money, passport, the lot.'

'People always do things for reasons best known to themselves, don't they, really?' replied Pearl. 'If you think about it.'

For reasons best known to herself the chief bridesmaid was emptying the remains of a pina colada over the bride-to-be's head.

'I turned down two fares to Gatwick on your account. Waiting for you.'

Tone lifted the little pink paper parasol from his drink, crushed it and dropped it into the ashtray.

'O-ooh, my little girl would've liked that.'

'She can have the cherry.'

Tone held it out to her, vivid green, dripping on a cocktail stick.

'Too sticky.'

'Wrap it up in a tissue.'

Pearl considered. 'Not worth it.'

She leaned forward and sucked the cherry, with a little explosion, into the moist red circle of her lips.

'Swizzle stick?'

'She's got a red one.'

'Well then.' Tone prodded Luke hard in the stomach with the plastic trident. 'I reckon you owe me for two runs to Gatwick, return fare, plus tips and my waiting time, in addition to your little trip – that sound fair to you?'

'Sounds fair enough to me.'

They all turned to Lemmy, who was leaning forward eagerly.

'Excuse me.'

Tone picked up the orange felt-tip from the wet table, uncapped it, leaned across, and wrote 'Can't you read?' under Luke's message on the plaster.

'Oi! Who d'you think you're . . . ?'

He slammed his cast between Tone's spread thighs. Tone screamed and clutched himself writhing and groaning. At the same time the fiancé of the girl whose hen party it was lurched past them, glassy-eyed and unbuttoned from his stag night at Busby's, dragging her by the arm to a foretaste of connubial bliss.

'Anthony, old chap. Just the man I was looking for . . .'

Jeremy Weasel, for reasons best known to himself, had been sinking a few pints in a remote corner, prior to going home, after a long day. He had attempted to engage in conversation an old chap in a cook's jacket, who looked like some sort of lascar, but his overtures had been met with such flat East Indian hostility that he had greeted the sight of Tone's familiar head, behind which he had travelled many times in the cab, with disproportionate pleasure. He clapped his hand in a comradely way on Tone's shoulder; Tone twisted round to lift tear-filled eyes to his face.

'Mr Headley-Jones. Did you want a cab?'

'When you're ready, Anthony. It's Mrs Slattery, isn't it?'

Jeremy addressed the neckline of her dress. Pearl made a cautious admission with a nod.

'We met once when I collected Ruth from playing with your daughter – Toffee Apple, or something, isn't it?'

'Tiffany.'

104

'Last orders! Let's be having you . . .' The bar staff were rattling the metal grille, like demented monkeys at the zoo.

'I'll be in touch, Sunshine,' said Tone, narrowing his eyes at Luke as he followed Jeremy to the door. Lemmy clanked out too, a bottle of Sanatogen, which must have added to his discomfort as he sat, protruding from his rear pocket.

'Well, Luke, I suppose we'd better be going too. You never told me you were German.' Pearl cast a regretful eye round the circle of empty glasses.

'Incha got no homes to go to?' a barmaid, temporarily stuck to the carpet by a piece of chewing gum on her cruel shoe, asked of the remaining crowd. An old woman in the corner gathered up four plastic carriers and an old music satchel splitting its sides, and emptying the ashtray into her handbag, shuffled out in front of Pearl and Luke.

'I may be old fashioned,' remarked Pearl outside, twining her arm through Luke's, who thought savagely that any old arm would have done to lead her through the summer night, 'but I don't really like people wearing shorts in public places, do you? I mean, you can be sitting on a bus and suddenly some great naked leg plonks itself down beside you. I think you ought to be given the choice whose flesh . . . The council ought to do something about these pavements . . . .' Then the thought of an unpleasant letter from the Director of Finance, Reigate and Banstead Borough Council, silenced her and turned her walk to a moody stomp.

Alone in the kitchen, Luke lit a Gauloise. Pearl had gone upstairs to check on Tiffany. He heard voices and the flush of the cistern, a watery starburst of sound on the ceiling. Somebody had cleared up the kitchen. The bulb shed a calm light from its dusty pleated-paper shade; clean plates waited as white and mild as Ursuline nuns in their rack on the draining board.

'You look very French.'

Luke closed one eye to avoid the twist of smoke from the thick white tube distending his lips. He saw that Pearl's remark was a compliment and in the joyful realisation that she had at last said something nice to him gave a crooked little half-smile at her across what had been transformed – the carnation stuck into an empty wine bottle on the checked oil-cloth, the dish of lemons, a coarse and heavy silver scrolled fork, the crumpled pack of cigarettes – into a café table top in France; a place which neither of them had visited.

'Coffee?' said Pearl as she tapped out a cigarette and struck a match.

'*Une demi-tasse, s'il vous plaît, madame.*'

'You make it, love.'

'*Avec plaisir, madame.*'

With such pleasure did Luke fill the kettle from the tap, the silver stream of water drilling into the thin aluminium, place the kettle precisely over the coronet of blue flames and place a spoon in readiness beside the jar of brown dust and chicory, in a feeling of intimacy stretched so tight that the slightest wrong move or noise would break it. He looked for thick white cups. 'You make it, love.' *Amour, chéri.*

He could not allow the two unsatisfactorily English mugs to spoil the illusion; there was a chipped green octagonal one, and Susan from Biology; this name had puzzled Luke until at last it had been explained that the mug was so named because it had been given to Cherry by a girl in her biology group. There was also a mug called Steven. Luke was gradually learning the family language, the Slatteryspeak. He knew now that the blue knife was a black-handled vegetable knife, the only knife that would cut properly and almost the only knife that wasn't blue; and that the Good Scissors, whose name must have been appropriate once, were the ones whose blunt blades were held together perilously by a loose pin, and when wanted, were never on the hook where family myth said they always hung. He had become used to Sally Slug and Trail the Snail and greeted their silver tracks in the morning.

'Where did you get these cigarettes?'

'Found them in the pub.' He forbore to add that they might have belonged to Tone. So far Pearl had given no indication that the evening had been in any way bizarre. He gave the mugs a cursory rinse, bearing in mind her fury when he had scoured the teapot.

'*Deux cafés*. Which one would you like?'

'Don't mind. Susan. No, the other one.'

'Have you ever been to France?'

'I almost went to Dieppe once. You?'

'I was going to go with the school once, but they wouldn't let me get on the coach . . .'

As he sipped his coffee, he saw the two of them seated at a little iron table on a clifftop, sipping absinth. He was wearing a white suit and a white wide-brimmed hat; Pearl was in black. Exiled. Beneath them the sea that must forever separate them from England.

'Elvis and Precious went to a hypermarket last year. You should have seen the stuff they brought back.'

Her words shattered his deliciously melancholy fancy. He did not want to be reminded of her children.

'Was Tiffany OK when you checked?' Perhaps if he mentioned her she would not, for once, appear and ruin everything.

'Sleeping like a baby. Curled up with Goblin.'

'Bless her,' said Luke, borrowing one of Pearl's favourite benedictions.

'Do you think I ought to get her a flea collar? She could wear it round her ankle, her legs have been quite badly bitten.'

'Good idea.'

'You should have seen the stuff they brought back. Litres of wine, beer, fags; a set of saucepans, a glass decanter and a punch bowl with little cups that hook on the sides . . .'

'Fondue set, cuddly toy . . .' added Luke.

Pearl laughed. 'What *was* that programme? Bruce Forsyth . . .'

'"The Generation Game".'

'They did bring back a cuddly toy. That big pink candy-floss-looking dog of Tiffany's.'

'They call it cotton candy in America.' They might have continued in this desultory companionable way, had Luke not suddenly driven his fist into his palm.

'What's up?'

'Nothing. Sorry.'

'I thought maybe you just remembered something.'

'No. More coffee?'

'I wouldn't mind a top-up. I suppose we ought to go to bed.' She yawned, stretching her fists above her head. 'What a day. That garden party . . .'

With his back to her, Luke poured half the blue liquid from the little bottle into her coffee. He licked a drop from his finger; it was tasteless, so there was no need to add sugar to mask any strangeness or bitterness.

'What did you think of him, my father, I mean?' he prattled nervously as he set down the mugs. 'You said you liked him . . .'

'Oh, he was nice.' The silver flask glowed in her memory. 'Sort of – good, if you know what I mean.'

'God,' said Luke. He raised his mug to her. His hand was shaking. Coffee slopped.

'*Salut,*' he said.

'Cheers.'

He watched her drinking. Now the love potion was flowing in a blue crystal stream down her oesophagus, into her stomach, into her bloodstream, turning her veins to liquid fire, her brain to a blue hydrangea, inflorescent with desire.

'I think I'll go up now.'

He washed his mug and turned for one last look at her, innocently licking a shred of French tobacco from her teeth, before she would be changed utterly.

'Goodnight. I don't suppose I'll go to sleep right away. I may read for a bit . . .'

He took the stairs three at a time, waving his fists above his head in a silent shout of triumph.

After a speedy shower, he dusted his damp skin with

108

sharp-scented talc from a rusty tin painted with freesias. As he pulled on his trousers he saw a sapphire heart, pulsating like the exposed ruby to which Our Lord points a sorrowing finger in holy pictures on the walls of devout homes, glowing against the bodice of Pearl's dress. He reached for his toothbrush; his hand was stayed by the sight of Pearl's, the oldest, as befitted her rank, its bristles splayed and tangled, its yellow handle flecked with calcified paste. A cruel little voice said, 'If you weren't in love with her, you would hate her toothbrush.' To silence it, he took Pearl's toothbrush, smeared it with toothpaste from the mouth of the flattened tube and applied it to his teeth.

As he folded the towel over the side of the bath the sight of his wet powdery footprints, grotesque and white, rooted him to the floor. He stood transfixed in the scent of freesias while the footprints, walking away from him to the basin, grew abominable: a yeti's tracks. The stairs creaked. He grabbed his shirt, fumbled open the door, and ran to his room, backing against the closed door as people do in the movies; his sweaty hands slithering on the wood. He saw Cherry's chaste bed, he saw himself and Pearl writhing on its surface, his fingers turned to pounds of uncooked sausages flailing at the buttons of her red and white spotted dress; terrified of what he would see if he did get it undone, under the gaze of Snoopy pirouetting on the wall. He didn't love her, he didn't even like her. She was bigger than him, she was too old, he wouldn't know what to do, he heard her mocking laughter as she sat up, pushing him away, pale and plucked, like one of those rubber chickens in joke shops. He hadn't even paid for that stupid love potion. The bill had arrived and was crumpled in a pocket. A tap was running in the bathroom. Where was Tiffany when he needed her? He strained his ears but his head was filled with the noise of drumsticks pounding the thin membrane of a tautly stretched drum. There was a knock on the door, and he was pushed forward as it opened.

'Luke?'

The rubber chicken squawked.

'I wonder if you'd mind occasionally turning out the bathroom light? Have you any idea of the size of the electricity bill? Goodnight!'

ELEVEN

*H*ELEN finished wrapping the personalised golf-tees she had ordered for her husband's birthday, and decked the little parcel with a rosette of ribbon. It was so difficult to think of things to give him; he had everything a man could want, including a Black and Decker, jump leads for the car, a de-icer, four or five key-rings and corkscrews, an army of shirts from Marks and Spencer, some still unworn, a foot regiment of socks, a dull cascade of ties, boxer shorts patterned in paisley, Madras checks and polka dots . . . She could almost wish that he smoked; it would make life simpler at birthdays and Christmas, except that she was so against the habit.

'Do you mind if I smoke while you eat?' her hostess had asked at a recent dinner party, when Helen had been slow to finish her second helping of Pavlova.

'Do you mind if I choke while you smoke?' Helen had replied, at her weaseliest, spoon cracking white shards of meringue.

Now, as she went to put away her little parcel she lifted up her head and sniffed; that ghastly smell of joss-sticks again. She had told Isobel about it several times. She must nag her again.

III

'This house smells like a bordello,' Jeremy had said only last night when he came in, laying down his briefcase and lifting his head to sniff the air in the way characteristic of his wife. She had been going to ask how he knew, but the alarm on the cooker had intervened. Bordello, seraglio; the words whispered silkily of heavy damask curtains making oriental dusk of languid afternoons, patchouli, pomegranates, epergnes of fruit, a white odalisque, and a slave with skin like a dark-bloomed grape fanning the scented air with ostrich feathers. Quite unlike the peeling establishment in Redhill up whose dank stairs she had once, mistakenly and innocently, toiled with her foil trays of Meals on Wheels. The dishes had been snatched by a woman in a petticoat and Helen had been left standing, still wearing her social smile, in the dark passage outside the slammed door; behind which, it seemed, a client was being entertained already to boiled cabbage and biscuits. She had never confessed, and a pensioner went dinnerless that day.

Brothel. That was a more suitable word for it, she thought as she reached for the *Guardian*, a place where they dined on a brownish broth made from old bones. She laughed, a short bark, and stopped, startled to realise that the face of the white odalisque of her fantasy was that of Pearl Slattery.

She turned quickly to the newspaper, seeking first the Women's pages, but on the way her eye was arrested by a small headline at the side of the Overseas News page. 'Thirty-Three to Hang.' She wished she hadn't seen it. She didn't want to know. She dashed for the kettle. The sheer number. It wasn't fair to spoil her morning; there was nothing she could do about it anyway. She would have to concentrate very hard on the logistics of her own day, and if she did, she knew, the horror would recede and if she did by any mischance, at the end of the day, remember the brief paragraph she could console herself with the thought that the thirty-three were already dead.

There was an interesting article on the revival in popularity of hand-knitting but, as she read, the skeins of wool kept twisting into ropes.

Imagine such an occurrence in Reigate, or Redhill: it would merit more than half a column-inch in the *Surrey Mirror*. Outside the Old Town Hall would be the best place, she mused, or the Priory Park, or on the roundabout near Redhill station; scaffolding and ropes erected in an obscene gymnasium on the grass. Pastoral scene of the gallant South-East. Helen shook her head violently to dislodge the image, and made herself a cup of coffee.

'Only instant, I'm afraid,' she apologised automatically, although she was alone in the kitchen. As she had not read the news item she had no idea of the nationality of those due to die, or of the reason for their sentence, but she imagined them to be of a brownish hue and had read recently that those who die for Islam believe that they will go straight to Paradise, and so she consoled herself.

She remembered that Isobel was at home, on study leave for her exams.

'Coffee, Isobel?' she called up the stairs. There was no reply. Helen climbed the blue-carpeted treads, taking pleasure in the silky feel of the banister she had stripped herself, and in the serpentine grain of the wood. If she had gone a bit over-the-top with the blue and white décor, so that the impression was rather that of living in a willow-pattern plate, at least it was clean and fresh. She paused at the landing windowsill to adjust by a fraction of an inch the position of a Chinese bowl and restore a fallen violet petal to the pot-pourri. Although she still made Ruth's bed every morning, she had, at Isobel's request, made it a policy neither to tidy her room nor to enter uninvited. Consequently, it was some days since she had crossed the threshold. She expected to find Isobel at her desk under the window, frowning into a textbook or staring vacantly into the garden, pen in mouth, long brown hair in studious disarray. She tapped on her white door, noticing that the ceramic plaque which said Isobel's Room, in a garland of forget-me-nots, had fallen off and disappeared, leaving two splintery holes.

'Darling, I . . . what on earth? . . . Where's Isobel?'

'Having a bath,' said Sean Slattery, not rising from Isobel's unmade bed where he lay, his boots in a tangle of sheet, a thin cigarette between his thumb and forefinger. The air was thick with smoke and sickening with the smell of joss-sticks; corrupt roses and jasmine. Helen crunched over dead matches and crisp packets and disembowelled cigarettes and switched off the schools' broadcast flickering on the little screen.

'I was watching that.'

She stood panting, taking in a burn mark on the duvet cover, the Whimsies on the dressing-table in a heap, thick with dust and splotched with candle-grease, the congealed fried egg and ketchup and ash on the Crown Derby plates on the floor. She seized the radio, to switch it off too, but achieved only a louder blast of music, on which she ran out in tears.

She sank down at the kitchen table in bewilderment and pain, weeping as she remembered Isobel's pleasure when they chose that Hollie Hobbie duvet cover and matching pillow-case together in Allders, not so many birthdays ago. She saw now that the ceramic plaque had not fallen from Isobel's door, but had been removed.

After a few minutes she blew her nose loudly, wiped her eyes and, literally, pulled herself together, tucking her blouse into the waistband of her skirt as she rose to clean the kitchen windows. Her grief turned to anger as she thought of that Slattery boy sprawling on the bed.

Shaking with rage she grabbed a cloth and a can of window polish, pressed the trigger, and sprayed the window savagely with a hail of spray.

'Christ, Mother, don't you care about the environment at all?' Isobel had come into the kitchen and was standing gesticulating wildly at the window. 'Don't you know you're destroying the upper atmosphere with that aerosol? I mean, God, look at this place! How many trees were cut down to make that kitchen roll? And as for –'

'Shut up! Shut up! I'm going out and I want that creature out of my house before I get back. *If* I come back –'

Helen ran out of the back door in tears and into the street.

Pearl went to Sean's room in search of his sheets for the launderette and staggered back in amazement in the doorway with a pile of dirty washing in her arms.

The Weasel lay back on Sean's bed, tears running down her face, a can of beer in one hand, a cigarette wobbling in her mouth, flicking a broken match on to the floor with the other hand.

'It's not fair,' she wept, the cigarette jerking wetly. 'It's not fair, I love her so much and all she, all she does is . . .'

'How much have you had?'

'Only this.' She waved the can.

'You must have a weak head.'

'I've given my life to her, not that I mind, I wanted to, and all she does is criticise – I think she must really hate me, and I love her so . . .'

'Who?'

'Isobel.'

'But what are you doing here?' Pearl stepped forward, letting the dirty clothes fall, and plucked the sizzling cigarette from Helen's lips.

'Well, your son does exactly the same in my house, so why shouldn't I? He puts his filthy boots all over my sheets and flicks his ash all over my floor and burns holes in things and . . .' she said looking up defiantly, and stopped as Pearl took a step towards her, hand swinging back in a slap of defensive motherhood.

'Don't hit me.' She cowered back on the bed drawing up her knees protectively, then, incredibly, Pearl's arm was round her and she was wiping her tear-blotched face with the corner of the filthy duvet.

The knowledge that she would have to break the news to Jeremy that Sean Slattery was to be present at his birthday dinner buzzed all day in a headache in a little zigzag vein on the periphery of Helen's bulgy brow. Twice she dialled Jeremy's

office to warn him and so deflect his rage on his homecoming;
twice she hung up on the switchboard girl, deciding that it
would be worse if he had more time to brood. The boy had
been sitting there, like some sort of pale insolent bean, at the
kitchen table, in a denim jacket with the sleeves ripped out and
no shirt, when Isobel had asked if he could accompany them to
the restaurant.

'But darling, it's Family . . . Daddy's birthday . . .'

'He won't mind.'

Isobel's face threatened sulks and refusals. The lout sat
there, breaking a match, with neither the grace nor the wit to
decline the invitation.

'Do you like Indian food?' Helen asked him desperately.

'Don't mind.'

Oh, God. He would probably order egg and chips.

'I want to go to the Chinky,' whined Ruth. 'I hate curry.'

'I've told you not to call it that. It's rude,' snapped Helen.

She had felt unable to refuse outright, after Pearl had been so
nice to her.

Then Sean had said that he had to go and sign on.

'Sign on what?' Helen had asked, but she found herself
driving those two able-bodied young people, whispering and
snorting in the back of the car, while Ruth prattled in the front.
All three seemed unaware of her fury. Surely she had dinned
into the children, from nursery school days, that they must
never invite a child in front of that child, without asking her
first. She noticed that the Co-op had closed down. If there was
some way that she could suggest that Sean should offer to
contribute to the bill in the restaurant, that might placate
Jeremy; but she knew it was impossible, and it would never
occur to the Slattery lout in a hundred years . . . Helen had to
brake sharply to avoid a small boy weaving across the road.
Sweat sprang out in her curly hair. She wound down the
window to tell him off.

'Don't, Mum.' Ruth pulled her arm in a torment of embar-
rassment. 'He goes to our school.'

'Glued out of his head,' said Sean. Ruth switched on the

radio adding a crackling of pop music to the heat, the fumes, the splintering electric drills that were blasting lumps of tar from the road.

'If you must have that thing on, let's have some decent music at least,' Helen shouted.

She switched to Radio Three. It was a cricket commentary. She admitted defeat.

'Shall I wait for you?' she said acidly, parking outside the DHSS. 'I'm sure you don't want to walk home in this heat?'

'Shouldn't be long,' said Sean climbing out and, of course, leaving Isobel to scramble unaided from her side of the car, slamming the door.

Helen hated sitting outside that building, its ugly architecture as shabby as the people who came and went. Scruffy, down-at-heel, it looked so – well, Slattery was the word that came to mind.

'Redhill's gone down and down,' she accused Ruth. 'It used to be quite a pleasant place. What was the name of that boy who nearly stepped in front of the car?'

'Denzil Pierpoint-Pratt. Or it might have been Tyrone, they're twins.'

Helen had been shocked at the children's matter-of-fact response to the child's condition. A tragic indictment of our society. She was going to have a word with the Headmaster tomorrow. Somebody had to do something. What sort of parents could allow it to happen? She tried to picture Mr and Mrs Pierpoint-Pratt.

'Are there any more children in the family?'

'There's Carly, she's in my class, and Damien, and Solange and Zak, and I don't know what the baby's called.'

'The mind boggles,' said Helen, with heavy humour. 'They're not related to the Slatterys by any chance, are they? Let me get this straight, you're telling me that walking round Redhill are a family named Denzil and Tyrone and Carly and Damien and Solange and . . . Zak?'

'Better'n Ruth.'

She pronounced her own name with such scorn that Helen sank back, wounded.

'Don't you like it?' she asked weakly, scratching at the body of an insect on the window.

'Petty bureaucracy!'

Sean and Isobel slammed themselves back into the Weasel-mobile. Isobel's use of her father's expression recalled the horrors to come to Helen.

'Did you get your Giro?' Ruth asked. How on earth did she know that word, a child of her age? It showed that she was mixing in altogether the wrong circles. Perhaps a change of school, before it was too late. What strange names common people gave their children. And yet Pierpoint-Pratt didn't sound common; not the first name anyway. Elvis and Cherry and Sean and Tiffany. The names flashed by like gaudy hunks of junk-jewellery. Pearl Slattery wasn't entirely common either; she was sort of – indefinable. What made it worse, somehow, was that that little glue-sniffer had been wearing a red and white football strip. She shivered at the thought of those brittle legs splayed from the wide white shorts under the wheels of the Range Rover.

'Can we drop Sean off?'

'Why not? Anywhere else you want to go? Any of you?'

'I just want to pick up a tape from Sean's place,' said Isobel, ignoring or unaware of the venom in her mother's voice.

Helen parked roughly outside the Slatterys' house, noticing the unkempt roses sprawling on to the pavement. Hadn't been pruned for years.

'I'm going to see Tiffany.'

'No, you're not! Ruth, come back!'

She was bounding up the crumbling steps.

'I was brought up to think that a gentleman opened a car door for a lady,' called Helen as Isobel followed Sean from the Range Rover.

'Mother! Must you *always* show me up?' Isobel hissed wrenching her leg from the brier that had caught it.

'Me show you up. That's a laugh,' Helen muttered miserably. She sat, wounded by her children, strapped to her perch above the hot pavement, feeling lonelier than ever in her life, as if the seatbelt was being pulled tighter and tighter, strangling in black webbing. A huge bumblebee blundered about at the open window; she watched it through blurred eyes, almost willing it to sting her. 'Damn Jeremy's birthday! I wish he'd never been born.' The bee decided to fly in. Instinctively she swiped at it with a rolled copy of *The Greensand Way*. It fell stunned to the road. She didn't dare look. She hadn't meant to kill it. She hadn't meant what she said about Jeremy. Damn. She punched the horn with her fist. It was echoed faintly by the chimes of an ice-cream van but there was no response from the Slatterys' house. She saw a grey rag of nylon net twitch at an upper window of the house next door, and wondered at its wormy Bed and Breakfast sign, and an old mattress rotting in the garden. What slimy writhing horrors would be exposed if one lifted it? She shuddered, as if she had raised its stained corner and glimpsed its vile underside.

'It's just not good enough!' she muttered as she strode up the steps, causing to shy away a passing little dark child. She couldn't tell if it was a boy or a girl. It wore trousers and its hair was gathered into a sort of muslin or Muslim white frilly bag on the top of its head. No one answered the door, which was open, and she stalked through to the kitchen.

Pearl was seated at the kitchen table in front of an untidy mound of buff envelopes. She swept them to the floor as Helen walked in.

'Look at these bloody bills! I don't see how anybody's supposed to live. And I'm having all sorts of stupid hassles with my Supplementary Benefit . . .'

'Doesn't anybody work for a living any more?' thought Helen. She was ashamed to catch Pearl's eye, but at least they were not alone. That shifty-looking boy, the so-called lodger, and why wasn't he at work, placed two mugs of tea on the table. Pearl pushed one towards Helen.

'Have a cup of tea.'

'No, don't . . .'

'Don't be so stupid, Luke, there's plenty in the pot. Pour yourself another.'

'Thank you. I don't mind if I do. I'm parched. What a day!'

Helen sat down and, wearily grasping the mug in both hands, took a sip of the tea and the second half of the love potion.

'Lovely.'

'It's a bit weak . . .' said Pearl.

'It's warm and wet . . .'

'And it gets you from A to B,' put in Luke.

The Weasel's face was already flushed but her neck was dyed a deeper pink.

'Does anybody stay in the house next door?' she asked. 'Bed and breakfast, I mean?'

'People come and go. There are two tortoises in the back; they're semi . . .'

'Literate,' said Luke.

'Wild, I was going to say. I don't really know the owner that well.'

'Were you looking for somewhere to stay, then?' asked Luke.

'I think you're an extremely rude young man,' said the Weasel, rising to her hind legs and draining her mug. She walked to the door and shouted.

'Isobel! Ruth! Come here at once!'

Luke and Pearl exchanged a glance.

It was Cherry who came into the kitchen.

'Oh, hello Mrs Headley-Jones.'

'Hello, dear. How's school going?' Helen smiled; at least one member of this ménage had some manners.

'Oh, not too bad, thank you,' she shrugged prettily in her cotton dress.

Cheap, but cool and pretty, decided Helen, of the dress.

'Can I make some sandwiches, Mum?' asked Cherry.

'What for?'

'Bible study picnic. I did tell you . . .'

'I wouldn't bother,' said Luke.

'Why not?'

'I heard that there's going to be loaves and fishes . . .'

'Leave some bread for the morning,' said Pearl. She turned to Helen. 'I never see her these days since she joined that church. She's always out . . .'

'I wish Isobel would do something like that. She's got in with a really awful crowd. Oh, sorry, I didn't mean . . .'

Sean, Isobel and Ruth came into the room.

'It's just not good enough,' scolded the Weasel. 'I've been kept waiting at least twenty minutes. Do you think I've got nothing better to do with my time than to chauffeur you about? Get in the car at once. Oh, Sean, these summer evenings can get a bit chilly, can't they? I suggest you put on a shirt tonight.'

'Goodbye, Mrs Headley-Jones. Thank you for coming,' Pearl called after her.

Helen's head popped back round the door. 'Thank you for the tea. Oh, by the way, I meant to ask, how are the clowns coming on?'

'Oh, I'm afraid I've only managed to do half a dozen so far . . .'

'Super! Gosh, you put me to shame!' With a patronising smile, the face withdrew.

From the hall came Ruth's piping voice: 'Mummy, why can't Tiffany come with us to the restaurant?' and what sounded suspiciously like a smack. The front door banged.

'What clowns?' said Cherry.

'Oh, just some clowns the Weasel forced me to say I'd crochet.'

'But you can't crochet.'

'Oh, I'll think of something . . .'

She scrunched the bills into a ragged heap and stuffed them into a handbag.

'I'd better get on with the tea. I've got to get to work later. Sean, are you in tonight, to keep an eye on Tiffany?'

'I'm going out with the Headley-Joneses, aren't I?'

'You're what!? You mean she asked you? After this morning?'

'Izzie did. *She* didn't mind.'

'Much! You must be mad. So that's what she meant about a shirt. She was afraid you'd disgrace her.'

''S'a free meal, anyway, innit?' He stuffed one of Cherry's sandwiches whole into his mouth, despite her squeal of protest.

'D'you think she'd mind if Gaz came along?'

'Oh no,' said Cherry, 'I'm sure she'd be delighted, the more the merrier.'

'So there's only you and me and Tiffany for tea,' said Pearl to Luke. 'What are you laughing at?'

'Nothing, really. Only the Weasel drinking her tea.' He went into the garden.

'Where are you going for your picnic, love?'

'Box Hill.'

'Well, be careful. It's very steep. Here' – she fished twenty-five pence from her pocket – 'get yourself some chocolate, or a can of Coke or something.'

Cherry's kiss was worth the cigarettes which Pearl would now forgo.

Luke had been in a funny mood all day, Pearl thought. Furtive, as though he had done something wrong, but she didn't know what. He'd gone to the launderette, though, when she'd asked, and hung the washing out to air. She hoped he'd bring it in, when she was out, so that she wouldn't have to put it away.

Luke flung himself on the grass. The recent rain had not done much to restore it. He remembered lying in the garden when he was small, feeling the world turn beneath him; he couldn't get that feeling now. His shame at last night's panic was receding. After all, no one knew of it but himself. He wrenched up a tuft of coarse grass and flung it. He had been a fool to believe that witch–doctor. He must have thought him a right idiot. His face burned. Love potion! He would send him the money as soon as his Giro came. No, he would take it round, pretend it had worked. That would show him. The clunk of shells came from the next-door garden. He laid his head on his arm.

'Luke! Tea's ready.'

Tiffany was pulling at his shirt.

'You're going to meet me from Majorettes.'

'Oh, really?'

'Mummy said so, so you've got to.'

She jumped on his back, winding her legs round his waist.

'Get off. I hate little girls who cling on to me.' He was forced to carry her in.

'I suppose I could always burn down the house,' Pearl was saying to Sean. 'Pretend they'd been destroyed in the fire.'

'Brilliant. Then we could claim on the insurance.'

'What insurance?'

Pearl banged glutinous loops, gloops of pasta, on to three plates.

'Or I could learn to crochet . . .'

She banged the bottom of the ketchup bottle.

'Bloody woman. I could kill her. What's it to her if that mattress next door is a health hazard? None of her bloody business.'

Red gobbets gushed on to her pasta.

'Hey. You two, you don't do anything all day – you could . . .'

The two boys shook their heads slowly from side to side.

'Oh, well. Sean, you make sure you offer to contribute to the bill tonight.'

'Supposing he accepts?'

'He won't.'

'I hadn't realised it was black tie.'

Jeremy Headley-Jones ran a hand over a chin still stinging from his birthday aftershave and stared at the apparition which, he had just been informed, was to join them for the celebration. It was wearing, over jeans, a dinner jacket that reached almost to its knees. The sleeves, rolled to display a dirty white silk lining, were pushed to the elbow.

'At least he's put on a shirt,' thought Helen, with a private little hysterical laugh at the marcasite cluster brooch that fastened the mean red and black tartan collar.

'Shall we have a drink before we go?' she said, the little bells on the drawstrings of her gauzy ethnic dress jangling nervously.

'You know me, never refuse a drink,' said Jeremy; the veins on his jowly face above the white sweater bearing him out.

'Sean, what will you have? Coca-Cola, Perrier, lemonade . . .'

'Um – what else have you got?'

'G and T all right, Sean?' Jeremy, salivating and impatient for his own long drink, elbowed his wife out of the way. 'Ice and lemon?'

'Cheers,' said Sean.

'Same for you, darling?'

'I'll have a small sherry, thank you.'

Taking it, pursing her lips, she said, 'Here's to Daddy. Happy birthday, darling!'

'Happy birthday, Daddy.'

Isobel and Ruth scowled at each other over their Coca-Colas.

'You can have a glass of wine with your meal,' said their mother sharply. 'Drink up, everybody. We'll be late.'

At least Jeremy had not hit the roof, about Sean.

The restaurant was empty.

The party entered too quickly and telescoped as Jeremy came to a standstill, between the two rows of tables waiting like brides in silver and white to be smirched with red and yellow. Ruth trod heavily on Isobel's foot, bringing tears to her eyes from the pain and from shame at her family's choice of a restaurant where nobody else wanted to eat.

'For five, sir?'

There had to be some shifting of furniture to accommodate Sean, who was left in no doubt that he was the extra.

'How nice, we can see the trees,' said Helen determinedly, when they were established. The trees from the Priory Park shimmered blue in the windows.

'You would say that.'

Isobel dismantled furiously the white cone of her napkin. Sean copied her.

'I beg your pardon?'

'You always have to say something. If we're sitting on the beach you have to say, "How nice, we can see the sea."'

There was silence but for the cracking of poppadums.

'Do you know what that picture is, darling?' said the Weasel to Ruth in a sugary, didactic tone. 'It's the Taj Mahal.'

Then she struck.

'Did you find that tube of Clearasil I got you, Izzie darling? I popped it on your dressing-table.'

Jeremy ordered four lagers and a Coke.

'You said we could have wine,' Ruth accused her mother.

'I don't think so, darling. Anyway, I don't think it really goes with curry.'

Ruth's answer was a rude noise with her straw.

Sean stared at the bristly creatures which had appeared on his plate. He suspected them of being tarantulas in batter.

'What are they?' he croaked to Isobel.

'Onion bhajis, haven't you had them before?' the Weasel replied.

'Oh, yes. I just didn't recognise them at first.'

'Please God make somebody else come in,' Isobel prayed.

How the waiter must despise them. Ruth was vociferous in her demand for egg and chips. Her father insisted that she should try some curry. Sean could not believe that people could spend so long discussing what they should eat. Helen and Jeremy conferred earnestly over their menus. The Slatterys would have cleared their plates and left by now.

'What are you having, young man?'

'Vegetable curry, please.'

'Try the chicken dansak,' suggested Jeremy, 'or they do very good rogan ghosh.'

'Sean's a vegetarian!' Isobel spluttered, 'and so am I. We don't eat corpses.'

'So am I,' said Ruth at once. 'I hate meat.'

'Isn't that rather like spitting on Grandpa's grave?' replied the Weasel quietly.

'Girls, girls!' Jeremy attempted to lighten the atmosphere. 'We're supposed to be celebrating. Everyone can have whatever they like.'

'Egg and chips,' said Ruth.

Her father accepted defeat gracefully. Isobel thought she heard their waiter mutter to another that he was not running a transport café but she could not be sure. She resisted her father's playful finger chucking her under the chin. Her knife and fork blurred, gigantic, and a tear blobbed on to her plate. She had been very fond of her grandfather and she remembered that she had not been to visit his grave in Redstone cemetery for years. He would think she had forgotten him, which was almost true, and that made it worse. She felt something soft pushed into her lap under the table, and found her father's handkerchief in her hand. He winked at her, and she blew her nose, resolving to take a bunch of flowers to the grave the following day.

'What about your B_{12}?' the Weasel suddenly fired at Sean.

'You what?' He gave an embarrassed snorty laugh that even Isobel could see was graceless.

'Where do you get your B_{12}?'

'Dunno. Safeway's, I s'pose,' he mumbled.

Ruth had fallen in love with the waiter. She smiled at him each time he set down a dish, and said thank you, to make up for the rest of her family's lack of manners.

'Mummy, aren't Indian people *nice*,' she said loudly. 'When I'm grown up I'm going to marry an Indian.'

Jeremy buried his face in his lager. Isobel tried to kick her sister and kicked her mother, who was looking at Sean to see how he reacted. The waiter, to Ruth's disappointment, gave no sign of having heard. Sean was preoccupied with another worry; he was afraid to lift his fork in case the mouth was the wrong orifice in which to place food. He had not observed the others eating their bhajis; perhaps they had placed them in their ears or their eyes or their pockets. Perhaps he had committed a gross obscenity. He tried to remember other occasions on which he'd eaten but his mind was a complete blank. He concentrated on the Taj Mahal.

'Ruth, do close your mouth when you're eating,' said the Weasel. That was no help.

Isobel's prayer was answered. The door swung inwards to admit a woman and a man. They were friends of the Weasel's and stopped for a chat at their table. Sean was not introduced; the Weasel could find no way of explaining that he was not Izzie's boyfriend. The members of the birthday party all relaxed now that they were not alone. Sean saw the others lift forkfuls of food to their lips, and was able to do the same. He even chose spoonfuls of pickle and chutney from the circular palette which the waiter was twirling at him.

'Do you see much of your brother?' the Weasel asked him conversationally, sucking a little bone and wiping her paws delicately.

'Quite a bit.'

'What does he do?'

Sean saw that it was not, after all, to be a free meal. He looked her straight in the eye. 'He's a limbo dancer.'

'Really? How fascinating. But there can't be much call for limbo dancers in Redhill, surely?'

'He works the northern club circuit. And he's in a band. The Reigate Ranking Rap Band. He does a lot of charity shows. For old people and the disabled and that,' he concluded, as the lime pickle brought tears to his eyes. He soused it with lager and wondered how he could get it, and a piece of tree bark, unobserved out of his mouth.

'Just put it on the side of your plate,' said the Weasel, who had of course spotted his plight. He blushed and obeyed.

Isobel was staring at him; she had thought Elvis was a bricklayer.

'I do admire your mother,' the Weasel went on. 'She's so, so . . . I mean, she copes so well. It can't be easy for her.'

'Mmm.' Sean sought refuge again in his lager.

'And those lovely little girls, the twins.' She had almost said piccaninnies but had caught herself in time. 'What are their names? I saw them in the town the other day.'

'Gemma and Grace.'

'Adorable. You'd never believe she was a grandmother, would you, Jeremy?'

Jeremy shook his head.

'She must have been very young when she married for the first time.'

'Gymslip mother,' agreed Sean.

They were saved by Ruth dropping her fork.

'Leave it! The waiter will get you a clean one,' her mother said sharply, loud enough for the waiter to hear. Ruth was mortified. She gave him her most dazzling smile as he handed her a clean fork, but he did not see.

'Are you swotting for your As like Izzie?' Jeremy asked Sean.

'On the dole.'

'Ah, I see.' Jeremy turned to Helen. 'Remember I told you we were advertising for an office junior? Out of twenty-nine applicants, eighteen turned up. The others hadn't the common courtesy to cancel their appointments; five were late, most of them looked like refugees from a jumble sale and two of them could hardly speak English. Makes you wonder, doesn't it?'

Isobel and Sean exchanged a look. Isobel blushed as the waiter removed the glossy ruins of their meal. How he must hate them.

'That would feed a family in the Third World for a week,' she said, to dissociate herself from the wicked waste, but the waiter did not acknowledge her.

'Remember it's your father's birthday. Don't spoil it.'

128

'It's all a question of economics, Pudding,' her father explained.

Isobel's compunction, or her father's pet-name for her, did not prevent her from ordering a pudding. The Weasel dissuaded Sean from his choice of fruit salad, on the grounds that it would be tinned. He opted, like Ruth, for ice-cream, but when he saw the glistening orange curlicues on Isobel's plate, he reached over unthinkingly, Slattery-fashion, to help himself to a piece, catching the Weasel and Jeremy exchanging a satisfied smirk.

'Makes you thirsty, dunnit?' he said, setting down his empty flecked glass.

'I think we'll have coffee now,' said the Weasel. She watched as Sean took out a green and gold tin, opened it, took a cigarette paper, filled it with tobacco, rolled a cigarette and placed it between his lips. Isobel watched, wondering if he would offer her one, daring herself to accept if he did. Ruth watched, fascinated. Jeremy watched, wondering if he would get away with it. As Sean put the match to the cigarette the Weasel said, 'I wonder if you'd mind not smoking, Sean?'

They fell into a moony silence over their coffee. The restaurant was filling up.

'Was it here or the Chinky where they found a dead cat in the freezer?' asked Ruth.

'Shut up,' hissed Isobel.

'What's the difference?' said Sean. 'It's no different eating a cat than a rabbit or a chicken or a cow. You wouldn't know anyway once it was curried.'

'That's enough!' said Jeremy.

Helen felt sick. She remembered how, when she had been carrying Isobel, the only way she had been able to stop herself from being sick in the car had been to imagine a large plateful of curry. Strange how the spices had soothed her. And when she was carrying Ruth she had craved for pickled gherkins and Jeremy had bought an enormous jar of them at a chip shop and after she had eaten two, she hadn't been able to look at them. They had stood for months on their tails like baby alligators in formaldehyde; forgotten specimens in an old laboratory jar. And the pains had started in a performance of *Under Milk Wood* at the Ashcroft, and she had had to wake Jeremy and leave the theatre to drive to the hospital. It all seemed so long ago. She felt she did not have the stature in her children's eyes that her parents had had in hers. No one would ever again think her opinion, her likes and dislikes, of paramount importance, find her little idiosyncrasies amusing and endearing. Jeremy had not even noticed that she had left half her pudding. It was like being dead. Like a fragment of a bad dream, the scene in Sean's awful bedroom floated into her mind, when Pearl had so disconcertingly put her arm round her and dried her tears and rocked her for a moment in her arms. Helen had sprung to her feet, and trumpeted like a lost elephant into her handkerchief, apologised gruffly, and fled. She had known that neither of them would refer to the incident again, but she was left with the sense of something warm and soft, lost.

'Well, what would you like to do, assuming you had a choice?' Jeremy asked Sean.

'I'm going to be a writer.' Sean named the first occupation that came into his head that could not possibly prompt Jeremy to offer him a job. Nothing could have been further from Jeremy's mind.

'Oh no,' cried the Weasel. 'Writers are dreadful people. I knew one once. They eat baked beans out of the tin with knives and drop cigarette ash everywhere.'

'I don't care much for this music, do you?' Jeremy remarked.

'I like it.' Ruth was ready to embrace the whole subcontinent.

'Mum doesn't like any music except boring old op'ra,' snarled Isobel.

'Oh, Izzie, that's not quite fair,' denied the Weasel archly. 'I've been known to listen to Radio Caroline on occasion . . .'

Isobel muttered something about ageing hippies.

'At least hippies weren't always sneering at other people. They believed in Peace and Love,' Helen retorted, surprising herself, and Jeremy, for she had never been remotely hippie. While the Stones played in Hyde Park she had been playing tennis in the Priory Park and the only flowers she had ever worn in her hair had been the chaplet of orange blossom that had circled her brow and had charmingly failed to restrain her springy curls on her wedding day.

Isobel imagined herself slipping quietly away from her friends, saying 'Thank you, but I'd rather go alone' and leaving them watching her, mysterious and sad, a bunch of lilies in her hand.

'Where's the loo?' asked Ruth.

'I'll come with you. Izzie?'

'Mother!'

Helen rose. Now was her chance to check the kitchens, but she was deflected by a waiter.

'Of course I love you, you stupid cow,' someone was saying desperately into the payphone as they passed.

'How about a brandy?' Jeremy asked Sean, man to man.

'What about me?' Isobel's voice was shrill at being excluded.

Jeremy ordered three brandies, another Coke and a crème de menthe for the Weasel.

'Oh Jeremy, you shouldn't have. I couldn't possibly after all that rich food. And I don't think those children should either. Whatever were you thinking of?'

'I'll have it if no one else wants it.' Sean reached over, and downed the liquid emerald in one gulp.

Half-way home they had to let him out of the car to be sick. Isobel had to cram a tissue against her face to hold in the horrible brandy. Wiping his mouth with his hand, Sean said through the window that he would walk the rest of the way; no one attempted to dissuade him. As the tail lights disappeared he realised that he had forgotten to offer to contribute to the bill. Well, in a way, he hadn't really had anything, had he?

★

As Pearl got ready for work she smiled to herself at the thought of Sean out with the Weasels. He had looked really nice, a credit to her. She heard someone at the door, and as no one else answered, she was forced to clatter down herself.

Two tiny boys in green jerseys and caps stood on the doorstep.

'We're collecting for the third Earlswood Scouts jumble sale.'

'Let's have a look at what you've got then.' Pearl plunged her hand into their black plastic sack. She pulled out a shirt. 'That'll do Sean,' she said. 'Haven't got much, have you? What's this book?'

'I don't think you're supposed to . . .' one of the boys said politely, in bewilderment.

'Oh, all right, you can have this cardi, it came from a jumble sale anyway.' Pearl peeled off her cardigan and dropped it into the sack.

'I'm telling Akela!' she heard, as they thudded down the steps, the bag bumping behind them.

In the kitchen she examined the book. Poems by Christina Rossetti, in letters of gold on mildewed purple vellum. It had a religious look about it; she thought she might clean it up and give it to Cherry, who had been very subdued since the house party. She set to work on the cover with the nailbrush, and as she scrubbed the book fell open and she read:

> Does the road wind up-hill all the way?
> Yes, to the very end.

She sighed as she patted it with the tea towel, hoping the water stains would fade as they dried.

Cherry was lying face down on her bed. Pearl crept across the room in case she was asleep. Then a tremor in her shoulder betrayed the fact that Cherry was crying.

'Cherry, love, whatever's the matter?'

She pulled her up and was confronted by a red face blasted and blotched with tears.

'What is it? You can tell Mummy, whatever it is.'

Her children's tears inevitably inspired Pearl's own. They started to roll as Cherry shook her head desperately.

'Come on, you can tell *me*.'

'I can't, I can't.' She gulped, her nose swollen like a maraschino cherry.

Pearl was in a panic of guilt, guessing that somehow she alone was to blame.

'Has someone said something to upset you? Is it your exams?'

Another shake of the head.

Pearl gently brushed back a lock of Cherry's hair that was glued to her face with tears.

'I brought you a present. Look.'

She held out the little book still damp.

'And there's a shirt downstairs you can have. It's quite nice, a small check, blue and beige, small collar. It's a bit sweaty under the arms but you could cut the sleeves off . . .'

Far from being comforted, Cherry flung herself face downwards again.

'Tell me what's wrong. I only want you to be happy.'

Cherry sat up, and through her sobs Pearl discerned the words: 'How can I be happy when people I love are going to go to Hell?'

Pearl dropped the book on to the bed and went out.

'Well, thanks a lot, God!' she said, slamming her fist into her own door. 'Thanks a bloody bunch!'

She flung herself down on her bed, sucking her bleeding knuckle, thinking of her night with Malcolm.

'Thanks a lot, Ruggles. Twenty quid. Twenty bloody quid . . .' But that wasn't why she was crying.

TWELVE

HELEN, breaking the rule, while Isobel was downstairs, stepped from the blue and white morning freshness of the landing into the scented twilight of Isobel's room. The curtains were closed, a towel draped over the lampshade to dim the bulb, which had been left burning. She dragged open the curtains and whipped the towel from the light. She felt sick.

She stormed into the kitchen where Isobel was making coffee, waving a plastic lemonade bottle half filled with dirty water, with a drinking straw protruding from its side.

'You've been burning those joss-sticks again after I've told and told you! And what do you mean by hanging a towel over the light? Have you taken leave of your senses? Are you trying to burn the house down?'

'It helps me to study.'

'Nonsense. And why on earth would anyone have a lemonade bottle with a straw stuck through it? What's it for?'

'Nothing. It's not mine. Someone left it here.'

'It looks like some sort of hookah.'

Helen dropped a handful of paper and tobacco on to the table.

'And why is the floor covered in chopped up cigarettes?'

'It's Gaz. He's very anti-smoking, so he buys cigarettes and cuts them up with a razor blade. You ought to approve of that.'

Helen suppressed an urge to slap her daughter's face. She sat down heavily.

'I feel as though I don't understand anything any more. I wish someone would tell me what's going on.'

An hour later she was sitting with a friend at a round table in Hunter's listening to the splashing of the little fountain, sozzled on sweet coffee and Danish pastries, watching the world, or Reigate, go by.

'Have you ever heard of something called skag?' asked Helen.

'What's that?'

'I don't know. Just something I overheard – one of the children . . .'

'Probably some sort of new dance craze.'

'Mmm. I expect so . . .'

'Seems a shame that Tesco's gone.'

'Mmm. I never went there myself but I know what you mean.'

Helen tried to tell Sally about the plastic bottle but it was too complicated.

'I don't like this summer,' she said suddenly. 'I don't know why, quite, I can't explain. Something in the air. I shall be jolly glad to get away in July. I feel I really *need* a holiday.'

'Me too.'

'What on earth?'

A youth with two balloons down the front of a black T-shirt, wearing a perilous red vinyl micro skirt and with black hair sprouting through the red mesh of his fishnet tights, hobbled past on platform shoes, clutching the arm of a priest with long blond hair.

'College Rag Week,' explained Sally. 'It's Tarts and Vicars day. Yesterday was Leather and Bondage . . .'

'That's exactly what I mean,' said Helen.

'Those two aren't very good,' said Sally. 'They could have made a bit more effort.' She pointed to Rick Ruggles and Cherry.

Helen decided to walk home by a circuitous route by way of Wray Common and then take the short cut through the alleyways. Her legs felt long and gangly, in need of exercise. She set off through the tunnel crossing to the other side to avoid the dank stench of the lavatories set in the wall, striding, arms swinging, past old men with sticks, old ladies with shopping trolleys. As she emerged into the sunlight she was startled by a scuffle in the crumbling chalk bank hung with ivy. A jay flapped upwards with a young bird in its sharp beak; she saw its pink and blue feathers, bright eye, evil; and a parent bird flung itself, squawking, demented, about the path, battering the air with its wings. It was all over in seconds, except for the desperate cries of the parent bird. Helen was shaking; it was as if the jay, cruel and triumphant, knew exactly what it was doing and the parent bird knew precisely the enormity of its loss.

Helen's jaunty gait was subdued as she continued unseeing past the gaudy flowerbeds, past the space where the old library had stood, past the statue of Dame Margot, over the level crossing and into Holmesdale Road, past Cullens with bedizened ladies discreetly buying gin, past the pretty little houses hung with quince and japonica, into whose windows usually she liked to stare, past a small purpose-built block of flats outside which she almost, in her preoccupation with the avian tragedy she had witnessed, sent flying a dapper little ginger-coloured man in a blazer who stood and watched her until she disappeared round the corner into Croydon Road. Two pigeons flew past her under the railway bridge whose grey iron interstices they made soft with their crooning; a perilous nursery for their eggs which often rolled on to the pavement below. Helen smiled, not knowing that those of them which did not end as smashed heaps of feathers on the road were to be attacked at night by the hired guns of the council.

Her meeting with Sally had left her dissatisfied. She felt an absurd sense of loneliness, as if half of her was missing, or someone who should have been at her side was not there.

'This is ridiculous,' she told herself. 'Women of my age don't go around feeling that half of them is missing.' But as the cloudless sky arched blue above the shining bushes on the common and the cars whizzed past on the road she felt more alone than ever; it was like a pain in her side, as if a twin had been torn from her flesh.

She whistled up Barley, her Golden Retriever, who came bounding through the bracken to her heels. Only, Barley had died four years ago. She must get a puppy. That would take her out of herself. She saw the puppy lying back in her arms, yellow forehead in babyish wrinkles, staring into her eyes with his dark unblinking eyes, black lips at her breast. She strode away from this shocking image, slapping and slapping the burrs from her skirt.

At home, she found the name of an animal rescue society in the classified columns of the *Surrey Mirror*. She did not ring their number. They might palm her off with a smelly old black dog, overtly male, its muzzle prickled with stiff white hairs, lolloping along on three legs. She clapped her hands. It limped off, glancing backwards over its shoulder with rolling white eyes, before it could defile the roses.

Perhaps a rescued greyhound? But they were so thin and you could see through their ankles when they stood against the light. Too delicate. And might it not make her look rather *outrée*? She pictured herself dragged down the road like a sledge, arms outstretched and wrenched from their sockets at the ends of the leads of two gaunt galloping greyhounds, flecked with saliva from their flying tongues.

No. Emotional blackmail was out. Far better to find a reputable breeder. Bracken, the pick of the litter. She could feel his weight in her arms, his pale golden paws like pussy willow lined with thistledown, his stringy little tail, too soon feathering to a magnificent plume. She put him down; enough cuddles for now, Bracken.

'Of course, you'll always be special, Barley,' she said aloud, guiltily to the air and to any eavesdropping ghost. She changed into her gardening clothes.

'I just think it would be crazy to get a dog now, just when the girls are a bit off your hands. Think of the mess, the damage, holidays, kennels . . . You could always get a job if you're bored.'

Helen and Jeremy confronted each other over the dining-room table; they were alone, the girls had eaten earlier.

'I've got a job. Looking after this house and the girls and you.'

Helen felt vulnerable, exposed and foolish while he sat opposite, mopping up the tomato sauce on his plate with a piece of bread.

'I wonder how many of your colleagues came home tonight to home-made pasta.'

It had taken her all afternoon to fashion and to stuff the little cushions of ravioli with meat, to crimp the edges; they had looked so good she had considered for a moment making washable stretch covers for them, and the sauce had been perfection.

'It's only food, though, isn't it?' He hacked another slice off Helen's home-made loaf, scattering sesame seeds, and wiped it round the salad bowl. 'I mean, you probably spent all day on this, didn't you, delicious though it is, and you can buy ravioli in cans, can't you? Wine?'

Helen shook her head. Jeremy refilled his own glass, which bore an oily imprint of his full lips.

'Hey, you're not crying are you?' Jeremy stood up and put his arm round her, scrubbing at her face with his garlicky napkin.

'You're hurting me. I'm always here when the girls get home from school. Do you think that counts for nothing?'

She pushed at his bulky chest.

'You're a wonderful mother, and a wonderful cook. Don't cry. You never cry. I couldn't ask for a better wife.'

'Do get off me, I can't breathe.' She felt as hard as a knife against his softness.

'It's not really that I want you to get a job; it's just that I feel that if you had something to channel your energies into, you wouldn't need a dog, or get so upset about silly things like that jay. Nature red in tooth and claw, you know . . .'

'Perhaps I should take a lover?'

'Now you *are* being silly.'

He mooched over to the dishwasher and watched her stack the dirty things.

'How strange that more people don't kill each other, when we spend our lives surrounded by lethal weapons. We turn them to benign instead of murderous use.' Helen was thinking as she stared at the bunch of blades in her hand, then looked round the kitchen. There was not a utensil that could not be put to injurious purpose: even the curtains could strangle. She was staggered at the sheer danger of life. Of course, my childhood was soaked in blood, she thought. But that was a ridiculous distortion. Daddy had been the gentlest of men. And yet he had spent his life dismembering corpses. When the shop closed for the day, Helen had loved to take a bucket of soapy water and sluice the blood and sawdust into the gutter, and sometimes she would arrange sprigs of fresh parsley between the white trays in the window, so that it looked like a little formal garden.

Her own garden lay outside the kitchen window, a flourishing tribute to her industry and skill. Her herb garden was the envy of her friends and the object of frequent despoliations; her parsley was a by-word.

'Come and sit in the garden. Let's talk.' Jeremy took her fist in his hand.

'All right, I'll just get the secateurs.'

Tender pink and yellow shoots of rhubarb nestled under their curly leaves. Helen picked off a slug and sent it flying

139

through the air, a small moist grey missile, over the fence.

'Ugh.' She wiped her fingers on the grass.

'I suppose you wish I was like Pearl Slattery, and fed you on tinned spaghetti and instant mash and white bread. I bet she even buys tinned rhubarb.' The ultimate condemnation. Helen herself was committing what to Pearl was almost the ultimate sartorial crime; she was wearing brown, holey tights under grey Crimplene trousers, and open-toed brown sandals.

They sat on the wooden bench. The grass was vivid in the light of approaching rain, the garden took on the aspect of a nineteenth-century English painting where storm clouds of a peculiar bright grey reflect in the silky clothes and imbue the still figures with unease.

'I wasn't trying in any way to undermine you, or belittle you,' Jeremy said. 'I only thought that perhaps you were bored, and a job might take your mind off yourself.'

'Off myself?' Helen was incredulous. 'When do I have five minutes to think about myself? You're impossible. I'm going in to help Ruth with her French.'

He watched her walk away on her grey legs, in her sandals, the handles of the secateurs protruding like a gun from a holster from her pocket, through the living tapestry of her own devising. She turned.

'What about my Meals on Wheels? The voluntary services would fall apart if it wasn't for people like me. Think about that. Life isn't all getting and spending.'

'No, but if Ruth's to go to Dunottar as you suggested tonight, we're going to have to find the money . . .'

'Well, that must be a priority. I'm worried sick about Isobel! And my interview with Ruth's headmaster was unsatisfactory, to say the least.'

'Izzie will be all right. All teenagers go through phases.'

'Well, I just hope your complacency turns out to be justified.'

Jeremy sighed deeply. As far as he could see, apart from a slight snappiness with her mother, Isobel was the dear, charming child she had always been. Now would be the time for a cigarette if he smoked. He recalled, and dismissed from his thoughts, Sean Slattery, and watched a cloud of midges above the compost heap, hearing the electric whine of a lawn mower, and faintly from the house, the sound of dishes washing themselves. Helen's disappearing sensible legs made him feel faintly sad. He stared into a prickly little shrub where, among a few withered tags of blossom, tiny green gooseberries were forming.

'Daddy?'

'Hello, Pudding. Come and sit down.'

'I can't, I'm just going out for a bit. I came to say goodbye.'

'Good idea. A break will do you good. All work and no play, eh? Good Lord, look at that – I always thought worms were hermaphrodites.'

'They have to exchange genetic information.'

'Well, they can do it somewhere else.' Jeremy picked up the writhing pink knot and it followed the slug over the fence.

'Bye then, Daddy.'

'Bye, Pudding. Don't be too late.'

'I won't.'

Isobel kissed the top of her father's head and, the remains of her building society account in her pocket, set off for the Castle Grounds, Reigate's Itchycoo Park, her newly washed hair catching the light, cascading over the shoulders of the sweater she had nicked from Benetton.

In bed that night Jeremy cleared his throat.

'Darling, I've been thinking. Now that the girls are growing up and don't need you so much, perhaps we could . . .'

'Don't need me so much? What about Isobel's A-levels? And Ruth . . .'

'Oh, forget it. I'm going to sleep. I've had a heavy day, and I've got a heavy day tomorrow.'

They lay under the duvet unmoving as two long-barrows in a Wiltshire field, visited on holiday. Helen decided to go to the Job Centre in the morning, to take the most menial job on offer. That would punish him. Bitterly, she pushed Bracken from her thoughts.

'This is silly, Helen. Why are we quarrelling?'

'*I'm* not quarrelling,' she replied. 'It's just that I feel fundamentally devalued. Undermined.'

'Utter nonsense. Anyway, how often does anybody appreciate anything I do? I don't always feel like getting on that bloody train every morning. You should try commuting from Redhill every day . . .'

'Men must work, and women must weep,' said Helen firmly. Then she started to giggle at what she had said. She found Jeremy's hand and squeezed it.

'Give us a little cuddle,' she said; but something implacably weaselly in her, even as they kissed, decreed that he would arrive home the following day to find her absent and a packet of instant potato, a tin of spaghetti, and a tin of processed peas awaiting him.

THIRTEEN

PEARL came flying round the corner, late for the morning shift, skidded in her loose shoes, one of which had lost its buckle, and slowed to a trot as she approached Snashfold's, and then to a walk. She was amazed to see a knot of women outside the factory; it was the first time that she had arrived before the door was opened. Bloody clock must have been fast; she had killed herself for nothing. She pulled a comb through her hair and brushed a dry mascara across her lashes.

'Good morning, ladies,' she said as she sauntered up to them.

'What's good about it?'

Tracey was crying.

'What's the matter? Why don't we go in? Have you lost the key?'

Ida pointed to a notice pinned to the door. 'Factory closed. Bye ladies. Have a Nice Day.'

'He's done a bunk. Bloody Barrie's done a bunk.'

'It's a lock-out.'

'That's illegal, isn't it?'

'What about our shop steward?'

'I thought you were?'

'Well, I'm not.'

'If a certain person hadn't dropped her nail-file into the butterscotch.'

'That plaster in the Jelly Teddies didn't help either.'

'Well, it's not my fault if those waterproof ones never stick!'

'Shut up, everybody,' Ida commanded. 'This is what we're going to do. We are going to break down that door and we are going to set up a workers' co-operative.'

'Right!'

'Yes!'

'Right. Me, Enid and Pearl, when I say three, charge. Out of the way, Tracey, you're useless.'

'Why me?' said Pearl, peeved at being picked. 'Mercedes is bigger than me.'

'She's all flab.'

'Well, thank *you*, Ida!' Mercedes turned on her heel. 'I've got a feller at home who's quite satisfied with me the way I am!'

'On the count of three. Ready? One, two, THREE, CHARGE!'

Their shoulders crashed against the door; they bounced back.

'Ouch, I've done myself a mischief.'

'It's barricaded from the inside.'

Pearl clasped her shoulder in silent agony.

'What do we do now?'

'Bugger this, I'm going home.'

'Wait you lot! Where's your solidarity? You're not going to let the bastard get away with it, are you?'

'It was a lousy job anyway. And lousy money.'

'That's not the point. Women have been on strike at the Singer sewing machine factory for fifteen years. Pearl, I thought better of *you*.' Ida caught hold of Pearl's arm as she tried to sneak away.

'Think of the Gdansk shipyard!' Ida called after the defectors, not releasing her grip on Pearl.

'That's in bleeding Russia, not Red'ill,' came back the response.

144

'If you stood on my shoulders you could break that window and climb in and open the door from the inside.'

'What with?' said Pearl unhappily.

'Your shoe. Or my crash helmet. Put it on your head and when you get up, smash the window with it.'

'With my head?'

'No, take it off first, stupid.'

The helmet was clamped over Pearl's head; Ida crouched down, and seeing that there was no escape, Pearl hoisted up her skirt and climbed awkwardly on to Ida's wobbling shoulders. Ida stood up. Pearl swayed perilously.

'Take your shoes off, you're killing me.'

'Keep still, can't you?'

Pearl bashed the window with the helmet which bounded off the glass, jarring her hands and she nearly toppled backwards.

'It's hopeless.'

'Try again. Hurry up, you great elephant, my back's breaking.'

Pearl swung the helmet and smashed the glass just as a reporter from the *Surrey Mirror* arrived with a camera followed by a police car. The two militants were driven to the police station where they were charged with causing criminal damage. Ida was jubilant; Pearl burst into tears.

Blinded by misery Pearl pushed open the door of the pub and walked into the dreary morning smell of wet ashtrays, and 'Seasons in the Sun' playing on the radio behind the bar.

'This is an unexpected pleasure!'

'It may be unexpected, Malcolm, but it won't be a pleasure. Make it a large one. I've come to the end of the line.'

'Ice and slice?'

'I don't care.'

'Is it that bad?'

'Worse.'

'Another?'

'Why not?'

She could see why not; it was 10.45 a.m.; she had the rest of the day, the rest of her life, until she was dispatched to Hell by Ruggles wielding a pitchfork, to get through; and the false friend winking in the glass had betrayed her before.

'Look at that cat!' Malcolm pointed. Cio-Cio-San was stretched out across the warm top of the perspex case containing yesterday's hot pot and pies.

'Bless her,' said Pearl automatically.

'Why aren't you at work?'

'Hollow laughter,' replied Pearl.

'Do you want to talk about it?'

'No. Thank you. I'd better be going.' She set down her empty glass.

'I got some holiday brochures. Do you want to have a look at them?'

'Not now, Malcolm. Wouldn't you say that Mercedes is a good two stone heavier than me?'

'Definitely.'

Malcolm pulled in his own bulk and managed for a few seconds to leave a half-inch gap between himself and the bar.

'Holiday brochures. That's all I need,' Pearl muttered as she stepped out on to the stained pavement among all the people who hadn't just been charged with causing criminal damage. The word brochure reminded her of a threatening letter she had torn up that morning, before running out of the house, from a mail-order company demanding payment for, among other items, that disastrous dress she had worn to that garden party, and the return of her agent's wallet. She never asked to be an agent in the first place. She never asked to be a militant. The picture that would adorn the *Surrey Mirror* bulged in gross close-up in front of her. She saw the man who had disconcerted the Weasel sitting on the steps of a bank, a newspaper shielding his dusty dreadlocks from the sun, a bottle of cider at his lips. She was tempted to join him.

As she turned into her own road she saw a removal van ahead of her. She wished it was outside her own house, carting them all off far away to a fresh start, but she knew she was trapped. The shadow of Jack fell over her; soon he would return; yet another person hulking around her making demands. He would expect her to be pleased to see him, when really never was too soon for her.

'Oh no,' she said aloud. The removal van was parked outside Arcadia. Those two ladies' things were being carried out. The front door with its glass lilies and storks was wedged open; a radio played Wham! in the empty hall. She ran past. She could no more have looked inside than witness a rape. Where were they going? Was one of them dead? She didn't want to know. She would never look at the house again. There had been no sale sign. No indication. Pearl felt a terrible sense of betrayal.

A motorbike lounged on the pavement outside her house. Two helmets had been dumped in the hall. Voices came from the kitchen. Pearl punched the chandelier and a plastic lustre broke. She couldn't even have a cup of coffee in privacy. Too sick at heart to speak to anyone she started to climb the stairs.

Luke caught a bus back from Reigate where he had been sent to renew Cherry's library books. He was mooching around the town trying to decide if he dared meet Pearl from work that afternoon. He saw him through the window of the Oxfam shop, stepping into a dead man's shoes. His heart lunged. He ran. He felt faint, drained of blood. He blundered into Forte's café and bought a cup of tea.

It wasn't Jack Slattery, he told himself. He couldn't be out yet, Pearl hadn't said anything. He hadn't seen his face. It could have been the back of anybody's black oily head.

'My nerves are shot to pieces,' he thought, sipping the too-sweet tea.

Then he saw a ginger-coloured face looking through the window and stared straight into the speckled eyes of Major Moth. Blood flooded back into his face; the hot tea raced round his veins as he sat waiting in a sweat of steam and shame as the little man pushed open the café door and walked to his table.

'You look hot, my friend.'

'Just a hot flush,' mumbled Luke. 'I was on my way to see you. To pay you what I owe you.'

'Well, here I am. But why didn't you drop in on your way to the library and save yourself a journey?'

Luke's mouth dropped open. The Major's face was as flat and amiable as a gingernut.

Luke handed him the money.

'Thank you. Well, when can I expect an invitation to the wedding?'

'You tell me. You're the one with supernatural powers.'

Luke stood up, jogging the table and slopping his tea. As he walked out he heard a volley of cracked laughter behind him. He hesitated. He wanted to go back and ask when the potion would work; if he stood a chance with Pearl. The thought of her made him ache, he wanted so much to hold her in his arms. It was getting worse. He looked through the window and saw the Major receiving on a thick plate a cheesecake, hung with streamers of coconut, and joining the lascar at a corner table, and walked on in his pain. He realised he had never found that lucky charm, the elephant in the bean. 'We all lose our charms in the end,' Pearl had said. He had certainly lost his.

The air was thick with traffic fumes and a heavy smell of vanilla, and a feeling of bad temper and people coming to the ends of their tethers. A child, dragged along by the arm screamed and screamed. A dog tied up outside Safeway's howled as if its heart would break. A few thick raindrops hit the dust. He saw the Weasel, her long legs scissoring the pavement. A hand grabbed him.

'I want a word with you.'

It was Lemmy, the youth in leathers with the broken leg, from the pub. He was sprawled against the window of the newsagent's, a can of Carlsberg Special in his hand. His long cast had been replaced by a bandage.

'Why did you have to write that on my cast? It made me look a right prick at the hospital. They was all laughing at me.'

'You were messing with my woman,' said Luke trying to

148

keep his voice steady. To his surprise Lemmy took him seriously and did not hit him, so he added, 'No one messes with my woman.'

'I was only being friendly. I didn't know she was your old lady, did I? There's no harm in being friendly is there?' he whined.

'Depends, doesn't it?'

'And then that other bloke had to add his little bit. The doctor couldn't keep a straight face. I thought he was going to cut my leg off.'

'It was only a joke,' said Luke, dropping his macho stance, and backing away. Lemmy slurped at his can and held it out to Luke, who shook his head.

'You refusing to drink with me?' Lemmy's tone was threatening.

'Anyway, it's off now, isn't it?' Luke indicated the bandage.

'I've still got to go to physio, haven't I?'

'Yeah, well, be seeing you.'

Luke walked away.

'Hang about, I've got some tickets for Motorhead,' he heard, then a despairing cry of 'Wanker!' as he ran.

Behind him Lemmy, stranded in his wasteland of loneliness, sprawled against the shop window with nothing to look forward to except his visits to physio, and signing-on, and a hand knocked angrily on the window telling him to get off the glass.

As Luke passed Pendered's he almost collided with the Weasel who was emerging with two large carrier bags. She had, as she had intended, visited the Job Centre, but the ambience, the cards pinned up there had filled her with panic. She had walked round once, straight-backed in her crisp navy, red and white shirtwaist, casting a quizzical eye over the vacancies, rather as she might at an amateur exhibition of local landscapes.

She breathed a sigh of escape into the threatening air as the heavy glass door swung closed behind her. As she hurried along she almost tripped over the extended bandaged foot of a youth with an empty can of beer beside him, and a fresh one in his hand. He shook the can, pulled back the ring, and fallout of froth showered the Weasel.

'Do you mind?'

'No. Do you?'

'Well, really!'

Then she saw that he was crying. 'Look here, if you've got a drink problem, I suggest you contact AA. You'll find their number in the telephone book.'

'I did. They was all pissed.'

'I find that very hard to believe. What utter nonsense. You should pull yourself together, young man.'

She had found herself outside Pendered's, and her Access card was in her purse.

'Where are you off to?' she said to Luke, startling him with a smile.

'Home.'

'I suppose you mean the Slatterys'. It's not really your home, is it? Give you a lift if you like.'

'Thanks.'

'The car's in Sainsbury's car park.'

'Shall I carry your bags?'

'They're not heavy, thank you. Just a couple of skirts and blouses and a cotton dress. I was really looking for something for Glyndebourne.'

Her bag buffeted him as they walked.

'I'll just pop in and have a quick word with Pearl,' she said, switching off the engine outside the Slatterys' house.

'She's not in.'

'What?'

'She won't be back from work yet. Thanks for the lift.' He was anxious to be rid of her now that she had served her purpose.

She drove away with an unaccountable sense of pique and disappointment as if, absurdly, the purpose of buying those clothes had been to parade and flaunt them in Pearl Slattery's disgraceful kitchen. 'Buggeration!' said the Weasel. It was the closest she allowed herself to swearing.

'Is that you, Luke?' Pearl's face, red-eyed, peeped round her door.

'You're back early.'

'Luke,' she heard herself say wearily, 'be an angel and go to the offy for a bottle of wine and bring it to my room.'

'The old devil. He knew all the time. It has worked,' Luke thought, grinning at the memory of his meeting with the witch-doctor. Then he stopped dead. The Weasel had drunk the potion too. Was that why she had offered him a lift, why she had seemed so put out when he didn't ask her in? She had driven off like a bat out of hell. Could he handle them both? He would worry about the Weasel later, he decided as he bought the wine. He was not going to mess up this chance with Pearl. He stopped at a florist and bought a bunch of pink and blue cornflowers.

Sean and his friends had left; the house was empty. Luke tapped on Pearl's door, balancing a bottle of Baton Rouge, a corkscrew, two glasses and a carafe of cornflowers. The door opened.

'Thanks, you're a pal.'
• She took the bottle, the corkscrew, one of the glasses, and shut the door in his face.

An hour or so later Pearl, in search of the sun, picked her way through torn cornflowers that surprisingly strewed the worn carpet outside her door, pink and blue like the round liquorice allsorts, her favourites, and teetered in a pair of sawn-off denim shorts and a shrunken halter, carrying a book, a glass of wine, cigarettes and matches, intending to lie on the grass, cultivate a tan, and forget the horrors of the morning.

The garden was full of half-naked bodies.

'Afternoon, Mrs S. Coming to join us?' Ruggles, stripped to the waist and wearing shorts, waved with the hand that was

151

not in a sling, from the centre of a circle of young people, including Cherry, who were all staring at her.

'I hope I'm not interrupting anything.'

'Not at all, Mrs S. We were just praying.'

Pearl became aware of the tight frayed edges of her shorts cutting into her flesh. She pulled in her stomach.

'Cup of tea, Mum?'

She saw that the teapot and mugs were scattered in the grass.

'I've got this Ribena, thanks.'

As she backed towards the house Ruggles called, 'I'll borrow a lawnmower and have a go at this grass one afternoon.'

'How very kind. Perhaps you'd like to do the front as well?'

'*Pas de problème*, Mrs S.'

'What have you done to your arm?'

'A bit of horseplay that got a bit out of hand, I'm afraid,' he grinned ruefully.

'Horseplay. At his age. Why couldn't he just go and get laid like everyone else?' Pearl thought, and then, thinking of Cherry, abruptly changed her mind. She just made it to the kitchen as her zip burst.

'This has got to be the worst day of my life,' she told herself, as so often before. She said a prayer of her own, that Cherry might be delivered from the clutches of Ruggles. What right had he to come here and make her feel fat and guilty in her own garden? She should have poured the wine over his head. She had to get the shorts off, peeling them with difficulty over her chafed thighs. She heard them trooping through the house, the front door closing, voices in the street, the screech of the mini-bus door.

FOURTEEN

IT HAD been a pleasant respite, the absence of Rick and his entourage on the House Party. It had been bliss to enter his kitchen in the morning and know that it would be free of Young Communicants cracking eggshells and jokes, to enjoy long lazy breakfasts in companionable silence with the Deaconess and old Boxall. The Vicar had repossessed his church. He had conducted, in sobriety, several services and found himself, for the first time for months, almost believing the words he spoke in its cool stone and marble and brass. Evensong had always been his favourite; the flickering candles; the Nunc Dimittis; pastilles of coloured light falling on to the heads of the three or four members of the congregation, the choirboys' faces floating above their ruffs in the dim light like aconites, not acolytes. This afternoon he sat enjoying a peaceful pipe in a back pew, in an incense of tobacco smoke and flowers and polish. The gilded pipes of the organ rose in majesty to the vaulted ceiling. The Vicar glided down the aisle, his skirts sweeping the polished brass plaques in the floor. He stood at the organ, running his fingers over the keys, and pulled and released the stops, puffing on his pipe. It was a tragedy that this magnificent instrument should have

153

been rendered dumb, humbled by the harmonica and guitar.

'"Eyeless in Gaza, at the mill with slaves,"' he said as he flicked a switch and swung his cassocked legs over the seat.

Rick and Cherry, entering the church, were petrified by the Wedding March from *Lohengrin*. They stood hand in hand like two stone effigies in the aisle as the music swelled and throbbed as if it would burst the church walls. Rick broke free and ran down the aisle shouting.

'Stop it! Get down, whoever you are!'

Cherry followed, retrieving a flipflop which he had shed.

'Come down at once, do you hear me? This is Church property! Oh – it's you.'

The Vicar lifted his hands from the keys and turned, his lips drawn back in a demoniac grin, as if he would swoop, screeching, on them like a vast black bat. Cherry clutched Rick's good arm.

'What do you think you're doing, you old bat?' Rick was shouting, dancing in rage in his shorts, his sling and one flipflop.

'Ssh, Rick, it's the Vicar!' she shook his arm.

'Not for much longer if I can help it. He's a disgrace. He's smoking. He's probably drunk.'

The Vicar switched off the organ and descended and strode silently from the church. Cherry handed Rick his flipflop and followed the Vicar.

She found him like a broken black umbrella left by a mourner against a tombstone. 'I'm sorry we interrupted your playing,' she said timidly. 'I thought it was very nice. I didn't know the organ worked . . . Rick didn't mean to be rude, I'm sure . . .'

'Rick did mean to be rude.'

Cherry was torn between a wish to defend Rick and pity for Luke's father. She felt a blush burn her knees, engulf her body and rise up her neck. The Vicar stared at this pretty child with face marbling pink and white confronting him among the graves. Something was crawling in his eyebrow. He shook his head.

'Who are you?'

'I'm a friend of Luke's,' she replied, seeing an opportunity to reconcile father and son.

'A Friend of Luke?' he repeated uncomprehendingly, wondering if this was some new evangelical sect.

'Your son. Luke.'

'Oh, him. Did he send you here?' he accused.

'Yes, he –' She was unable to lie. 'No,' she admitted, 'he doesn't like me coming here, but I'm sure if you . . .'

The Reverend Ichabod Ribbons bared his teeth in a yellow silencing smile.

'Excuse me, I hope you don't mind me mentioning it, but there's a ladybird in your eyebrow. It's about to fall into your eye.'

He shook his head but could not dislodge it.

'Hold still. I'll get it.'

Cherry extricated the insect, which in flying away revealed itself as tiny and black and yellow instead of the enormous scarlet bug he had imagined as she fumbled in his wiry brow.

'Thank you, young woman,' he said, embarrassed at the proximity of her freshness to his soiled nicotine-stained person.

'That's one of the many unpleasant penalties of growing old. Your eyebrows turn into brier patches.'

As he turned his head she saw a rosette of thistledown in his ear. He stomped away towards the house sweeping a trail of old squashed yewberries and leaves behind him. Rick was on his knees as she re-entered the church. He held up his hand for her to wait.

'I've asked God's forgiveness for losing my cool,' he said when he rose. 'We had a good old chat.'

'Oh, good. What about the Vicar though?'

'I asked God to forgive him too.' Rick remembered the time when he had been singing 'Give me oil in my lamp, keep me

155

burning . . .', and the Vicar had said, 'You get on my wick, Rick.'

'Poor old man. After all, it is his church, Rick.'

'It's God's church, Cherry.'

'Yes, I know, but he wasn't doing any harm, was he? Why shouldn't he play the organ if he wants to?'

'It's the principle of the thing.'

Cherry felt rebuked. She could not see what was the principle.

'Why don't you put your flipflop on?'

'The thong's broken. Do you think you could fix it?'

'Let's have a look. No, sorry, I can't.'

She felt she had failed again. They walked together towards the gate. Rick took her hand, singing softly as they walked,

> '"If I was a wiggly worm,
> I'd thank the Lord that I could squirm . . ."'

He gave Cherry's hand a friendly shake but she squirmed and could not join in the song.

'Would you like me to retie your sling before I go? It's a bit loose. I think I'd better be going home.'

'Thanks.' He stooped and submitted to her. 'Bless you. Would you mind if I dropped you off at the station? I've promised to see a lass who's on the verge of anorexia.'

'Of course not.'

Cherry felt a stab of jealousy. She wished she had anorexia. Then she felt ashamed.

'Cherry, there's something I have to say to you. I've prayed about it . . . Don't think I'm getting at you, or criticising, but I don't know if you've noticed that most of the girls in Taskforce don't wear earrings.'

Her hands flew to her burning ears.

'My mum gave me these for my birthday. She'd be ever so hurt – anyway if I don't wear them the holes will close up,' she said almost defiantly.

'Think about it. It's your decision entirely,' he said quickly, leaving the thought to corrode like cheap metal in flesh.

Cherry was slumped in gloom as she waited for forty-five minutes on a platform packed with tired, hot, hungry and bad-tempered people for her train which had been delayed by a signalling failure outside East Croydon. She didn't know why she felt so depressed. She took a copy of *Buzz* from her bag and started to read, wondering as she did if she would be able to go to Greenbelt, the Christian pop festival, later that summer. Lots of her new friends had been and they made it sound great. Except for the latrines. She wondered if she could ask her mother for the money that evening. Maybe a holiday job. She did do quite a bit of babysitting but it was for members of the Church Family so she didn't get paid. As she read she twisted her earring until her ear was sore.

Rick knelt in the centre of his room, the lino cold under his bare knees. He prayed for the Slatterys: for Tiffany, that she might be persuaded to join Pioneers, the junior section of Taskforce; for Sean, that he might find some purpose in life before he destroyed himself; for Luke, that he might return to the Church Family. There *was* love in that house, he could see, but it was not the love of the Lord Jesus. He prayed for Pearl, that she might . . . his hand pressed on his eyes, he fell into a purple trance in which Pearl, weeping with repentance, broke a jar of precious ointment on his feet and dried them with her hair. He jumped up and put his Adrian Snell record on the turntable of his old Dansette record player, bought at a jumble sale. A previous owner had pasted a coloured picture of Ricky Nelson inside its lid; Rick had superimposed a *God Rules OK* sticker.

He was shaken at the way Satan had sneaked into his head while he was praying. He must be more on his guard.

He had been thrown by the Wedding March because it pre-empted his desire that one day he and Cherry should walk together down the aisle to that music. The age difference between him and Cherry worried him. He was encouraging her to go to university, she had much to learn, but knew that she would come under all sorts of influences there; he had observed the effect she had on the youths of Taskforce, of which she seemed quite unaware. He had told her that she must join the CU as soon as she arrived, and was comforted by the knowledge that they would be the first university society to seek her out, but somehow, before she left home, he must earmark her for his own. Earmark? Did that expression derive from those metal tags one saw in the ears of cows and pigs? He remembered her earrings and sighed.

The Vicar's hand shook as he splashed sherry into his Brasso mug. He had experienced a rare happiness as he played the organ, a sense of peace and a feeling that there might, after all, be a hope of redemption for him. Ruggles must go. It was how to get rid of him that was the problem. He could not risk involving a higher authority; in any confrontation Ruggles would have the congregation on his side. He could see himself, battered suitcase in his hand, a rope halter round his neck, towing his wife in the bath down the Vicarage path. He pulled a book from his bookcase; *Beside the Bonnie Briar Bush* by Ian MacLaren. That sentimental old Master of the Kailyard School could always be relied on to provoke the hot tears that he could not shed for his family or flock.

It was thus in an attitude of penitence, head in hands, weeping noisily over a heavy black book, that Rick found him when he came to apologise. He crept out and closed the door quietly. Outside he danced in glee, giving the thumbs-up sign to Heaven, hampered by his sling.

'Nice one, Jesus,' he said.

Lying in her bath, staring at the lower half of the frosted glass window, staring at its steamy snowflakes pocked with black mould, counting the bobbles that hung from the faded brown blind that fringed the upper panes, Jocelyn Ribbons had a strange perception of the outside world. Downstairs she could hear a faint humming and dull bangs as someone bumped a hoover into the skirting boards. An aeroplane took on the tone of a giant hoover and she fantasised an enormous angel cleaning the clouds.

The pile of towels on which she slept was neatly folded in the airing cupboard; her husband's old checked dressing-gown in which she wrapped herself at night was hanging on its hook on the back of the door. Soon the Deaconess would place her supper tray outside the door.

Occasionally, as now, the realisation that she must some day emerge would surface, like a slimy sliver of soap or a bloated fish. In the winter the house was freezing. The pipes might burst as they had before, or the boiler might explode or go out. She shivered at the thought and turned on the hot tap. Was she imagining it, or was the water not as hot as before? She floundered in panic. Had the fuel supply run out? Could her husband afford no more? Perhaps old Boxall had chopped down every tree in the churchyard and garden, and the Vicarage stood naked to the elements among truncated stumps. There were some wooden crosses in the graveyard but there might be unpleasantness if he used those, and there was lots of heavy antique furniture in the Vicarage that would burn well, but she supposed no one would have the wit to utilise it. The horror of having to see people, to speak, to do things. She submerged her body and reached over the side to switch on 'The Archers'. She did not care for it so much now; there were too many newcomers; she could remember when Tony had been Young Tony, and Young Lilian had galloped about Ambridge on a horse called Pensioner.

There was no powerpoint in the bathroom. It occurred to her that if she had a little electric fire, she could plug it into the light socket and balance it on the rim of the bath.

FIFTEEN

THE sound of 'Sylvia's Mother' informed Cherry that tonight would not be a good time to ask her mother for the money for Greenbelt. She found her in the front room dispiritedly dusting.

'This duster's disgusting. Remind me to get a new one.'

'Couldn't it be washed?'

'You can't wash them, they turn everything else yellow.'

'If it was washed separately?'

'You don't think I'm going to pay for a whole load just to wash one duster? It's cheaper to buy a new one.'

'I meant by hand.'

'You do it then, if you're so keen.'

Pearl flung the black and yellow rag to the floor. Cherry picked it up.

'I'll get tea, you look tired.'

Pearl regarded her suspiciously through puffy lids. 'Are you being nice because you care, or are you being Christian, or do you want something?'

'I don't know,' Cherry answered truthfully. 'What are we having?'

'Whatever. I might as well do it myself if I've got to decide what we're having. The twins are coming. They're staying the night, Elvis and Precious are going out.'

Pearl's conviction that this was the worst day of her life was strengthened at tea-time when Tiffany announced that the Majorettes were going to do a show.

'We've all got to have costumes,' she said. 'The mummies are making them.'

'I'll make yours when I've finished crocheting those clowns.'

Her heart was palpitating; she shuddered at the thought of food and longed to crawl into her bed, pull the covers over her head and surrender to blackness. Goblin leapt on to her knee, thrusting his face into hers. The whiskers lacerated, his purrs drilled through her head. Cherry had made the table pretty with a bunch of blown roses, whose petals fell each time someone jogged the table. Pearl watched the progress of an ant. Her dull brain took in the fact that Grace and Gemma were wearing belted brown dresses appliquéd with capering yellow hobgoblins, and she had not admired them.

'We're being enrolled next week, Nan, will you come?'

'Try and stop me.' The proud grandmother, handcuffed to a warder, in a dress of broad arrows.

'I want to be a Brownie,' said Tiffany. 'Can I, Mum? Ruth is.'

The massed thighs and bugles and batons of the Majorettes was bad enough.

'I'll see.'

'Cherry,' said Sean, 'is it true that you like Cliff Richard now you're a Christian?'

'Oh, leave her alone,' snapped Pearl. 'Where's Luke?'

'He's gone out.'

'Luke never goes out.'

'Go and fetch him down, Cherry.'

Luke, pale and red-eyed, was led in by Cherry.

'Izzie wants to know if you want to go out with her,' Sean greeted him.

'Go out?' Luke repeated. He couldn't go out. He had to stay

within Pearl's ambit. Going out with girls was in an irrecoverable past. 'I thought she was going out with you?' he said.

'He's going out with Gaz,' said Tiffany.

'Izzie and I are just friends, that's all. Well, what shall I tell her?'

'She seems a nice girl, Luke,' said Pearl, 'very pretty.'

'She's not my type,' said Luke desperately. He would not look at her. It felt like a conspiracy.

'We all know who is,' said Sean earning himself a slap round the head.

'Put the telly on,' said Pearl, her hand stinging from contact with her son's scalp.

'Did you know that there are detector vans in our area?' said Cherry.

'They won't get us. Nobody knows we've got a telly, seeing as they both came from the dump.' No doubt that would be the next blow. 'Turn the sound down,' Pearl said, 'there's no point in inviting trouble.'

'Are you working tomorrow night, Mum?' Cherry asked.

'No, I'm not. Why?'

'It's the sixth-form Parents' Evening.'

'Oh, good. I'll be able to come, then.'

What on earth could she wear? If only all the other parents didn't look like contestants from 'Ask the Family'.

The rest of the family had disappeared. Luke found himself alone in the kitchen with Sean. His once prospective son-in-law. He uttered a bitter, cynical laugh as Sean helped himself to a post-prandial snack. He had realised early in his acquaintance with the Slatterys that he must reconcile himself to their habit of sticking their fingers into jars – peanut butter, jam, mayonnaise – if he was to be able to eat at all. Even Cherry had a rare lapse, although now she blushed as if she had violated some Article of the Church if she caught herself at it. Pearl hit them if she noticed a finger in a jar, but she seldom did notice, and occasionally, alone and worried in the kitchen, unable to sleep, reading and rereading the free newspapers and junk mail that bombarded the hall, she succumbed too, especially when there was no bread. Usually, though, she used a knife or spoon. Sean was licking at the interstice of his fore- and middle-finger, which was clogged with Marmite. Dissatisfied, he ran his hand under the tap and wiped it on the tea towel. Then he drank from a bottle of milk and wiped his mouth on the tea towel. Luke compressed his lips.

'There won't be enough for the morning,' he said prissily, instead of voicing his true, on hygienic grounds, objection.

'There's another pint in the fridge.'

The refrigerator was an enormous obsolete Kelvinator whose loud motor had long since ceased to throb. That morning Luke had noticed that it was crammed with goodies.

'How come your mum manages to buy so much food?' he asked. 'I mean she's always short of money, even with what we give her . . .'

'She's got a friend at Safeway's, on the checkout.'

'Who?' Pearl was not allowed to have friends about whom he did not know.

'You never talk about anything except Pearl, did you know that?' Sean stared at himself in the bowl of a spoon. 'I'm really worried,' he said.

'It hardly shows.'

'What does?'

'Your spot.'

'I haven't got a spot. You want to take a look at your own face sometime. And why don't you do something about your hair? It's a mess.'

As each of them knew the other had no spots the conversation faltered.

'Worried about what?'

'I think I might have a narcissus complex. I was reading this article. You only think about yourself all the time, you don't relate to other people except in how they react to you. It's a pathological defect. Do you think I'm like that?'

'How should I know?' Luke answered suspiciously. 'Why, do you think I'm like that, is that what you're trying to say?'

163

'It's me I'm talking about, not you.'

'Yes, well, it would be, wouldn't it?'

Gaz's voice came down the stairs. 'Sean, you making that tea or what?'

Sean sighed and plonked a tea bag into each of two mugs and filled the kettle then, worried about his narcissism, turned to Luke. 'You having a cup?'

'OK. Do you think Pearl wants one?'

Sean rolled his eyes as he dropped two more tea bags into two more mugs. 'What shall I say to Izzie then?'

'Tell her – tell her I'll think about it.'

Just his luck that the potion had worked on the Weasel and not on Pearl. And now he was being pestered by her daughter as well.

Pearl switched off 'Coronation Street' as Luke came in with the tea. The scenes in Baldwin's factory reminded her too painfully of the morning's events at Snashfold's. Luke sat down. He had resolved never to speak to her again, and here he was again, racking his brains for something to say.

'I see that house down the road's been sold,' he offered at last.

Pearl slammed down her mug and left the room.

SIXTEEN

A PIECE of the grey thundery sky had lodged itself in Helen's brain in a cloud of pain over her eye. Jeremy lay peacefully beside her, but she knew she wouldn't be able to sleep. The broderie anglaise straps of her nightdress chafed her skin like a rough halter. She pushed off the duvet and lay wishing that the storm would break. The bedside phone rang like a flash of lightning. She grabbed the receiver, her thoughts flying to her children, but they were both in bed.

'Hello?'

'I have a call for you from a Reigate callbox, will you accept the charge?'

'Who on earth, certainly not – yes, I suppose so.'

'I'm putting you through, caller.'

Hoarse sounds came through the receiver. A heavy breather. And she had paid for the call. She was about to slam down the receiver when her weaselly nature prevailed.

'Look here, whoever you are, I'm having this call traced, so you'd . . .'

'It's me. I'm in a callbox.'

'Pearl? Is that Pearl?'

'Yes. I'm sorry. I just wanted to talk to you. I'm sorry. I'm going now . . .'

'Wait, don't hang up.'

Jeremy was sitting up, groping blearily for his lightswitch.

'I can't talk now, Pearl. Listen, I'm going jogging in the morning. I'll pick you up. Seven-thirty? Right.' She put down the phone.

Jeremy was blinking in the light. 'Who was that?'

'Nobody, darling. You've had a dream. Go back to sleep.'

As Pearl stepped out of the stained and smelly callbox a dull boom of thunder rolled round the sky and she was flattened against the broken glass panes by a fusillade of hailstones. Then she bolted for home, the attack of the elements driving from her mind the enormity of what she had just done. She had always been terrified of thunderstorms since her sister Violet had almost been struck by lightning the day their mother had disappeared.

'We were looking for you,' Tiffany accused. The three little girls stood hand in hand, wide eyed with fear in her bedroom.

'Never mind, I'm here now. You can come into my bed.'

With much scrabbling and squealing and squabbling as to who should be next to Pearl they at last found their positions. They were all elbows and feet; it was like being in bed with three large mice, sandwiched between two of them. Each time the thunder crashed the bed exploded in screams.

'Keep still,' groaned Pearl. 'I've got to get some sleep or I'll die.' She would have to run away, it was the only solution. Everybody would be better off without her.

'Are you crying, Nana?'

She hugged the little body close.

'Only because I'm so tired. Go to sleep.'

'But I'm scared.'

So am I, Pearl thought. She was shivering. She would go to her sister Belda's convent. They would have to give her sanctuary. She would become a nun.

'Mummy, you're shaking the bed!'

166

'Sorry.'

'She's tickling me!' Grace wriggled in ecstatic torment.

'Shut up.'

The house rattled. The thunder and lightning were very close together. There was a tremendous crash. Something in Redhill had been struck. Cherry appeared like a spirit of the storm illuminated by blue electricity, clutching the cat.

'I thought Goblin might be scared.' She put him down on the bed and climbed in beside Gemma.

'Your feet are freezing.'

'Go to sleep,' begged Pearl.

They lay packed together like pilchards in oil. Pearl remembered her flight to the Weasel with a suppressed groan. She had lain sleepless on her bed for hours, demented with despair and Helen had been the person she had thought of to run to.

'Cherry, aren't you ashamed of yourself, in Mummy's bed at your age?' It was Sean's mocking voice. Then at a particularly violent crash he dived for the bed.

'There's no room! There's no room!' cried the little girls.

'I'll go up this end.'

'I'm not having his feet in my face! Mum, tell him.'

'Oh, stop fussing. There's room for everybody. Now, for God's sake, let's get some sleep,' she said through Goblin's fur; he had settled on her face. Something wet and cold broke on her head: the roof was leaking.

Luke woke sweating from a dream of a nuclear holocaust. For a moment he was glad; then he realised it was a thunderstorm. His room blazed with jagged light. There was a barrage of rain outside the window, a sluicing, sucking, gurgling in the gutters and drains. Pearl! Suppose she was scared? Suppose she was struck by lightning? He ran to her room and flung open the door.

They were all sitting up in bed, all the Slatterys squashed together, awkwardly balancing mugs of tea on their hummocked knees, laughing at him. Even the cat. He stood in his underpants, blinking.

Cherry took pity. 'Want some tea, Luke? You can share mine.'

'No room, no room!' shouted the little girls as he approached the bed. He felt more than ever before an outsider, totally excluded, lonelier than ever in his life.

'Move up, Sean,' Cherry commanded, 'there's room for one more.'

'The more the merrier,' said Pearl, laughing weakly.

He crept in beside Sean, and hid his face in Cherry's tea.

'Why have you got that plastic bag on your head?' he asked Pearl.

'Roof's leaking. Look out, there's one just above you.'

He ducked; the water hit the tea.

'This is the worst storm I can remember,' said Pearl. 'I do hope Precious and Elvis are safe home. I wish they were here.'

'They'll be OK, Mum,' said Sean. 'They must have got back hours ago.'

'Of course they must,' she agreed, patting a granddaughter's leg reassuringly. The nun's habit fell from her. She knew then that she would not be able to leave her family.

'I hope the school's been struck!'

'I hope the YTS has been struck!'

'I hope the A-level papers have been struck.'

Luke and Pearl could not articulate their hopes. Luke hoped the witch-doctor and the Weasel's house had been struck.

'I hope the police station and the Gas Board and the Electricity Board and the Water Board and the Unigate Dairies and Reigate and Banstead Borough Council and the Majorettes and the Janet Frazer Mail-Order Company and the Brownies and the SDP, the sixth-form Parents' Evening, and all crochet hooks and Jack and Malcolm and Ruggles and St Elmo's Church have been struck,' thought Pearl.

Gradually the storm, soused by the torrential rain, fizzled out with an occasional flare and firecracker, and fitfully, after a fashion, they all slept.

Luke was woken by the closing of the door. He sat up. He

found himself where he had for so long wanted to be. Beside Pearl, in her bed. The only fly in the ointment was Tiffany who slept, thumb in mouth, beside her sleeping mother. His heart was beating so loud he thought it must wake them, but they slept on. He sensed that it was very early, although birds were twittering outside. He eased himself diagonally across the bed until he was beside Pearl. He could feel the heat from her body. His lips, light as a moth, alighted on her white shoulder. He grazed his finger down the hollow of her spine. He slid his hand under the sheet and found her breast.

'What the hell's going on?'

Jack Slattery, hair a dripping mess of rain and Brylcreem, water spouting from his shoes, strode across the bedroom, dragged Luke from the bed, picked him up and flung him through the door. He landed on his back, where he lay winded, his moment of bliss shattered, all his hopes ebbing away.

Luke ran to the station, his face a mass of tears, his arm bleeding from a gash from an out-flung rose as he fled, with pain like a thorn in his throat; the memory of his arrival, when Redhill had been all shimmering, a jagged lump of golden glass lacerating his chest at every step.

Behind him Pearl was slummocking around the kitchen in her tinselled dressing-gown frying breakfast for Jack Slattery, someone was making toast and 'Breakfast Time' was blaring and he wanted to be clasped to her quilted breast and she didn't care, didn't even, nobody, nobody, nobody . . .

The station looked deserted, too early for a train. Two taxis were parked on the forecourt. Luke dragged open the door of the first, kicked in his bag, and without wiping his face, slumped into the back seat. He said the first place that came into his head:

'Stoats Nest Lane, Coulsdon.'

Tone turned, leaning over the back of the driver's seat, a gold ingot nestling in the dark hairs of his chest, his mouth full of gold.

'Shall we go the quick way, or the pretty way?'

Goblin leapt from the bed, Tiffany backed out of the room.

'And I thought yesterday was the worst day of my life. What's the time?'

'Nearly seven.'

'I've got to get up, I'm going jogging.'

'I come home to find a man in bed with my daughter and my wife, and she tells me she's going jogging!'

'It wasn't a man. It was only Luke,' she yawned. 'When did you get out?'

'Yesterday. I wasn't going to come back when you didn't answer my letters, but I had to see you, Pearl. You're lovelier than ever. Let's go back to bed.'

'Are you mad?'

She saw his face darken and dodged. She went down to the kitchen and put on the kettle. Cherry was already there.

'Mum, can I borrow your jeans?'

'No.'

'Why not?'

'Because they're straights on me and baggies on you. Anyway, I'm wearing them, I'm going jogging.'

Cherry gasped as Jack Slattery came into the kitchen. She backed against the draining board. He dropped his raised fist.

'Hello, love. Got a kiss for your old Dad?'

She went forward dutifully, as rigid as the draining board.

Pearl made tea and went to dress. She came back into the kitchen. Jack was seated at the table in his vest, rolling a cigarette. She noted that his bust measurement had grown. There was a peremptory hoot outside.

'Bye.'

'What about my breakfast?' bleated Jack incredulously.

'Get it yourself.'

The morning, all dew and golden, as if it hadn't a care in the world, hit Pearl as she ran painfully down the steps in Sean's plimsolls. Helen, seated at the wheel of the Weaselmobile,

flashed white teeth at her as she climbed in; the whites of her
eyes were clear; no traces of tears and Baton Rouge there. She
was wearing a red tracksuit and, wholesome as a scarlet runner
bean, started the engine.

Steam rose from the wet ground and dissolved in the clear
sunshine as they ran.

'Hang on a minute.' Pearl grabbed the back of Helen's
sweatshirt to stop her pounding shoes, and they tumbled
together into the leaves. When they had disengaged themselves they sat side by side on a decaying stump starred with
vivid emerald moss.

'Doesn't the air smell wonderful?'

'Wonderful.'

Pearl inched a flattened pack of cigarettes from one pocket
and a box of matches from another. 'Want one?'

'Perhaps I will.'

Helen placed a cigarette between her lips. Pearl struck a
match. It was a wonder the box did not ignite spontaneously.

'I'm getting a puppy. I'm going to call him Bracken, what
do you think?'

'Nice.'

From far away came a cuckoo's call.

'What did you want to tell me?'

'You'll hate me.'

'No I won't.'

'Promise?'

'I promise.'

'I – I can't crochet!'

'It doesn't matter. I've left the SDP. Turn round, your hair's
full of twigs.'

Back on the road; an airship hovering ahead of them against
the blue, a huge benign presence emanating calm and goodwill
and hope; lolloping along in a sheen of sweat, Pearl caught
Helen's hand.

'"Does the road wind up-hill all the way?"' she puffed.

'"Yes, to the very end."'